East Sussex Coastal Railw

Volume 2: Branch Lines and Other Railw

Paul O'Callaghan

First published in 2012 by S B Publications
Tel: 01323 893498
Email: *sbpublications@tiscali.co.uk*
Website: *www.sbpublications.co.uk*

ISBN 978-1-85770-366-5

Layout by Vital Signs Publishing - email: *info@vitalsignspublishing.co.uk*

Acknowledgements

First and foremost I must thank my mother, Christine Weedon, for supporting me (due to my ill-health) on some
of my walks. I would also like to thank Peter A Harding for providing me with the railway photographers. Of the
railway photographers and suppliers of old railway photos, I would like to thank: Rod Blencowe (of the Lens of Sutton
association), Sue Bowman (of Seaton Tramway), Bob Cookson, Richard Casserley, Alan Davis, Hugh Davis (of Photos
from the Fifties), Alex Forbes, Mick Funnell, Roger & David Haggar, Hastings library, Lawson Little (of the Narrow
Gauge Railway society), Roger Quantril, John Scrace, John Spencer (of THWART) and the Transport Treasury.
In addition, I would also like to thank Jo Kirkham, and Lindsay Woods of S B Publications.

*[Front cover: H2 Class loco (working RCTS Tour Train) on the turntable at Newhaven. Photo: Photos From The Fifties.
Title page: Train at Volks Electric Railway, Brighton, August 2009. Photo: Andy Thomas]*

CONTENTS

Introduction, 5

PART 1: Main Branches
and Nearby Narrow Gauge Branches

1: The Kemp Town Branch
The History, 7; The Route, 9;

2: The Seaford Branch
The Background, 10; The Seaford Extension, 11; Keymer Junction, 12; Plumpton, 13; Cooksbridge, 14; Southease and Rodmell, 16; North of Newhaven Town, 16; Newhaven Town/Railway Wharf Line, 17; Newhaven Harbour Station, 18; Tide Mills and First Bishopstone Station, 22; Bishopstone Second Station (Current), 22; Seaford, 23

3: Newhaven West Quay Branch
Background, 25; The Route, 25

4: Eastbourne's Other Railway - The Crumbles Branch
Background, 28; Roselands (Waterworks, Gasworks, Electricity Works Junction), 31; Seaside Road Level Crossing, 32; Queens Crescent and Wallis Avenue, 32; The Crumbles, 32; Electricity Works Branch, 33

5: The Rye Harbour Branch and Narrow Gauge Railways
Background, 34; Rye Harbour's Private Railways, 35; Further History, 36; Other Nearby Lines, 37

6: The Dungeness/New Romney Branch Line
General History, 38; Construction and Opening, 39; Brookland, 42; Lydd, 43; Dungeness, 44; Lydd-on-Sea and Greatstone-on-Sea, 45; New Romney, 46; Fish Railways, 47

PART 2: Tramways and Other Small Railways

7: The Rye and Camber Tramway
Background, 49; General History, 49; Opening Day, 50; Rye Tramway Terminus, 54; Golf Links, 13; Camber Sands, 13

8: Hastings Miniature Railway and the Cliff Railways
Hastings Miniature Railway, 56; Hastings West Hill Lift Railway, 58; Hastings East Hill Lift Railway, 59

9: The Eastbourne Tramway
Background, 60; Extension of the Tramway, 62; Problems Arise, 63; The Final Years, 65; Aircraft Factory Line, 66

10: Hall & Co. Narrow Gauge Line
The Hall & Co. Line, 67; The Royal Artillery Line, 67

11: Volks Electric Railway and the 'Daddy Long Legs' Line
Volks Electric Railway, 68; The 'Daddy Long Legs' Line, 73

12: The Cuckmere Valley Railway
The Early Years, 75; The Post-War Period, 75

Appendix: Additional Photographs, 77
About the Author, 81

New Romney Station, 17th October 1929, with the 3.08 train to Appledore.
Photo: H C Casserley

Introduction

In Volume 1 of *East Sussex Coastal Railways*, Paul O'Callaghan explained his fascination with the important Ashford to Brighton railway line and the background to his own involvement in researching its intriguing history, following its path station by station across the county.

This second volume explores some of the numerous other lines which branch off from, or run near to, the main Ashford-Brighton route, including both full and narrow gauge railways, some of which have rarely been covered in print before.

The details contained within reveal a rich history of lines, many now lost to us, which have helped shape the regions and communities around them and played a crucial part in the development of East Sussex's transport infrastructure. These railways, or simply the memories and remains of them, deserve to be celebrated and remembered, preserved for posterity.

Enjoy the journey.

Newhaven Harbour Station, 11th October 1933, with the 10.05 from London Victoria.
Photo: H C Casserley

PART 1: Main Branches and Nearby Narrow Gauge Lines

Chapter 1: The Kemp Town Branch

The History

This railway was created as a strategic blocking move by the London, Brighton & South Coast Railway (LBSCR) to protect Brighton from being invaded by another railway company. Kemp Town, the eastern suburb of Brighton, was developed by Thomas Read Kemp, a Lord of the Manor of Brighton, in the early 19th century. The London, Chatham & Dover Railway (LCDR) supported a company which proposed to connect Beckenham in Kent (where the LCDR main line passed through) with Brighton. The LBSCR was alarmed at having its monopoly on serving Brighton threatened. Although the House of Commons rejected permission for the LCDR line, the LBSCR decided to propose their own railway in the Kemp Town area, to block other companies from building there in future. Local gentry had been calling for a line here for some years.

The LBSCR eventually gained permission for their line to be built on 13th May 1864, for a price of £100,000. The engineer was their own Frederick Dale Bannister, working with George Parker Bidder, and the contractor was William & Jonathan Pickering. The line was to be one mile, 32 chains, long. Much of it was built on brick viaducts, before going through a tunnel to reach Kemp Town. The railway opened for business on 3rd August 1869, although the official opening took place three days later. The Mayor,

Golden yellow-painted Terrier 0-6-0T A1, Class No. Ds377, named Brighton Works (originally No. 35 Morden, built 1878), at Kemp Town with SLS special train on 23rd June 1956. The loco was scrapped in 1963.
Photo: H C Casserley

The carriages of the special train, 23rd June 1956 (picture, previous page), photographed as the loco ran around them. Photo: H C Casserley

who laid the first brick, would also return to lay the last brick in the viaduct over Lewes Road. A meal for guests was held at the *Old Ship Hotel*, with ceremonies and toasts. (A full two-page account of the opening day, and the openings of the other Kemp Town stations, can be found in Peter A Harding's book, *The Kemp Town Branch Line*). The station at Lewes Road (next to the viaduct) was opened on 1st September 1873.

Due to the competition from the tramways being installed along Brighton's streets, the LBSCR introduced a petrol railcar (like the steam railcar that ran between Rye and Hastings, as explored in Volume 1) and opened a 'halt' for the service, with a new timetable, at Hartington Road on 3rd January 1906. However, this was done without informing the Board of Trade (halts had to be inspected before being opened to the public), the LBSCR believing that because the halt was the same as the other BoT-approved ones built along its lines then Hartington Road Halt wouldn't need individual permission. That, at least, was their defence when the BoT challenged them on it. Luckily, when the LBSCR invited the BoT down to inspect the halt two days after opening, it was found to be satisfactory. However, all this fuss was somewhat a waste of time as, in June 1911, it was closed, as the petrol train did not work well. It was replaced by a traditional steam loco and carriage.

All services on the Kemp Town branch eventually ceased from 1st January 1917 as a war time economic measure, and would not restart until 1st September 1919. Freight services would not return until 2nd January 1922, although by then Lewes Road had been reduced to halt status.

After the Southern Railway took over, activity ceased from 1st January 1933 (with the last train running the day before), due to a lack of passengers. On 29th July 1933, the Kemp Town Branch was re-designated as a goods siding!

Yet as a goods stop, Kemp Town Station remained much in demand. From May 1941 until October 1941, EMU (Electric Multiple Unit) trains were stored in the Kemp Town Tunnel to protect them from Luftwaffe bombs. On January 8th 1963, however, a disaster did occur when a locomotive ran through the buffers at Kemp Town and crashed into the building.

The line was finally closed on 6th June 1971, marking it with a final day passenger service every hour using a DMU (Diesel Multiple Unit) from Brighton. The local council bought the line, and the Hartington Road bridge was demolished in 1973. Today, Lewes Road Station and its viaduct has a Sainsbury's store on the site, while the tunnel mouths are now sealed up. The Freshfield Industrial Estate now resides on the site of Kemp Town Station.

Of the engines used, there were three 0-6-0T A1 Class Terrier locomotives that operated the Kemp Town branch: No. 41 Piccadilly (built 1872), No. 63 Preston (built 1875), and No. 64 Kemptown (built 1874). From 1901 until 1904, the LBSCR scrapped some of their 50 Terriers as they were now surplus to requirements, selecting those which required repairs to their fireboxes and/or boilers. This was the fate of Piccadilly and Kemptown. Preston survived until 1925 when it too was scrapped. Hornby have issued three models of Terriers, one of which is of Piccadilly and

the other of Martello, the real version of which now lives at Bressingham Museum. Other surviving Terriers can be found on the Bluebell, Kent & East Sussex and Isle of Wight steam railways.

The Route

The route of the Kemp Town Branch began at the junction of London Road Station (the route from Brighton to London Road is described in Volume 1), just east of Ditchling

Kemp Town Station, 23rd June 1956. Photo: H C Casserley

Tunnel. It passed a 19-lever signal box and was double tracked. Lewes Road Station had a different platform layout to most: between the two tracks was an island platform, but the up track also had a platform on its east side. This had the station building upon it, while a footbridge linked the platforms. A signal box stood at the south end, east of the down track. After the passenger services closed, only the station building, platforms and up track were left.

Beyond Lewes Road, the double track merged into a single and passed over the Lewes Road 14-arched viaduct and then over Hartington Road's three-arched viaduct, passing the halt. The line then entered a cutting (now filled in, with a playground on top) to enter the 1,024 yards-long Kemp Town Tunnel, before emerging into Kemp Town Station.

The station itself had a single track emerging from the tunnel, fanning out to 17 sidings, to the left and right of the station. The signal box at the tunnel mouth (like that at Lewes Road) was closed when passengers ceased. There was a long 481 ft platform, with a canopy (removed when redesignated as a goods siding), a bay platform and, at right angles to the platform behind the buffer stops, the station building, which was the twin of London Road, even down to the front steps. It survived until 1971.

Chapter 2: The Seaford Branch

Background

The Seaford Branch Line is the only regular passenger-carrying branch in South East England (Bognor Regis and Littlehampton are short, and treated as part of the main line). As related in Volume 1, the legal powers to construct a branch line to Newhaven were left unused until the BL&HR made use of them to reach Lewes. The Act of Parliament which gave permission for the construction of the railway to Newhaven also allowed the creation of the Eastbourne and Hailsham branches in 1846. The Newhaven line was primarily built to serve the port, hence it runs down the east side of the River Ouse, and not the west side to the town.

The connecting Wivelsfield to Lewes link line was authorised back in 1845, its purpose being to reduce the distance for trains between Hastings, Lewes and London, enabling them not to have to travel down into Brighton and back up the main line to London. Although authorised the year before the Newhaven branch, the link opened to goods traffic on 1st September 1847 and to passengers on 1st October 1847, just two months before Newhaven, which in turn opened to passengers on 8th December 1847 (goods trains had started running the month before), albeit operating with just a single track.

Terrier loco No. 32636, built 1872, with E6 Class 0-6-2T at Seaford, both having hauled the RCTS Railtour train from Brighton, 7th October 1962. The Terrier is now on the Bluebell Railway. Photo: H C Casserley

The LBSCR had wanted their own steamer boat service, but legal difficulties prevented this. However, as mentioned, as the link line was also built to enable trains to and from Newhaven and London to go direct between those places without passing through Brighton, its existence was more than justified. Along some parts of the railway, high walls were erected in areas where it ran near Turnpike roads (by order of Parliament) so that the locomotives would not frighten horses!

The Seaford Extension

Although plans for an extension to Seaford were submitted in 1845, no further action to obtain permission and construct one was undertaken. It appears this was due to concerns over a lack of financial backing. A London-based landowner, Reverend W Tyler-Smith, and another gentleman, Thomas Crook, began to promote the idea of an extension, as they had available land at Seaford, ideally to be sold to a railway company or housing developers who would come to Seaford if a railway was eventually built. In October 1860, a Mr H Simmons chaired a meeting at Seaford Town Hall to discuss the extension, and pointed out that a railway would halve the journey to Newhaven. The two landowners, who by now had sold the land for Seaford Station to be built on, attended the meeting, where Tyler-Smith announced he had obtained the support of the LBSCR for an extension to Seaford. This meeting was followed by a press advert announcement of the new Newhaven & Seaford Railway.

The extension was finally opened on 1st June 1864. F D Bannister supervised the construction, with W Bannister as engineer. The opening day was accompanied by a dinner and speeches at Seaford, while Reverend Tyler-Smith became vice-chairman. Interestingly, as the LBSCR had said it could only pay for two-thirds of the construction, the final third was paid for not by local Seaford people, but by a group of gentlemen in Lewes. The Newhaven to Seaford line was expanded to double track on 24th July 1904.

In 1886, the Eastbourne, Seaford & Newhaven Railway Company was formed to propose extending the Seaford branch across the Cuckmere Valley and the South Downs (by unspecified means – perhaps by tunnelling), onto Eastbourne. Unsurprisingly, there was little enthusiasm for such an expensive railway, so nothing more happened, following a report of a meeting in 1891. Another proposal was put forward to extend the Seaford line up the Cuckmere Valley to Wilmington on the Eastbourne to Lewes line, but that too received little support. From 1914 until 1924, there were further proposals (in adverts for the new housing development at Peacehaven) to construct a branch line from Newhaven to Peacehaven.

On 4th July 1935, the line was electrified for electric trains, which then started on 7th July. The Luftwaffe attacked the Seaford branch during World War Two. On 3rd July 1940, a train approaching Bishopstone Beach Halt was machine-gunned by a German plane, killing the driver. The fireman managed to take over the train and drive it to Newhaven. In 1941 a substation (for electricity to the third rail) was bombed, putting the electric trains and signalling out of action.

The line reverted to single track from Newhaven to Seaford in 1975. A lot of the history of the Newhaven and Seaford railway is tied up in the various branches which split off from the Seaford line in Newhaven, and will be dealt with here as part of the route of this line.

The Route

i) Keymer Junction

This is where the link line running south to Lewes begins, just south of Wivelsfield Station. The location of the

Unit 7366, Brighton to Victoria, passes Keymer Junction where the link line from Lewes joins the Brighton main line, 28th April 1971. Photo: John Scrace

junction has given the beginning of the line a tight curve, and a signal box once stood on the east side. Ten chains south of the junction (along the link line) is a level crossing, which not only had its own signal box on the south side of the crossing, but was also accompanied by Keymer Station, which existed here on the north side of the crossing from 1862 to 1883, when it was replaced by Wivelsfield Station. Beyond here, on the north side of the link line, was Keymer Brick & Tile Works, which at one time had its own siding (this had been removed by 1974). Another signal box once existed at Spatham Lane crossing.

Plumpton Station, 2006. Photo: Paul O'Callaghan

The crossing keeper's house at Plumpton, 2006. Photo: Paul O'Callaghan

ii) Plumpton

Opened in 1863, Plumpton Station is now a statutory listed Grade 2 site, including its up platform shelter, signal box (on the south west side of the crossing), and even the 1910-erected footbridge, as well as the weatherboarded station building (believed to have been built as late as 1890) on the down platform. Unusually, the signal box has a spike upon its roof. A cattle dock was located at the north (London) end of the station, with a goods siding behind the down platform.

Signal box, with roof spike, Plumpton, 2006. Photo: Paul O'Callaghan

A crossing keeper's house exists beside the now rare old-style gates level crossing on the west side. In 1910, an extra up platform (now very overgrown) was constructed beyond the second footbridge, which connects a footpath with the down platform at the north end. The famous Plumpton Racecourse lies immediately west of this attractive station.

ABOVE: Cooksbridge Station, looking south towards Lewes, 1950s. Photo: Hugh Davies/Photos From The Fifties. BELOW: Approaching Cooksbridge on the train from Newhaven to Victoria, 24th April 1937. Photo: H C Casserley

iii) Cooksbridge

Although the original station building (on the down platform) has been altered and expanded over the years, especially in 1894, the up platform shelter here is one of the best examples in Britain, upon which models should be based. Indeed, when the planned Unicorn Retreat Centre residency opens and establishes its own narrow (miniature) gauge railway, its Permaculture Halt is to have a mini-replica of this very shelter. It is unusual in that it is a surviving example of a shelter with a chimney. In fact it is even more

Cooksbridge goods shed, now in private use, 2006. Photo: Paul O'Callaghan

ABOVE: Cooksbridge's up platform shelter, with chimney, 2006. BELOW: Inside the shelter, showing the fireplace. Photos: Paul O'Callaghan

use as a business. A siding once left the goods yard to serve a private timber yard, although housing is now planned to replace the whole site. A level crossing at the station's south end had a signal box on the north side into the 1970s, but it has been demolished since. Further south was Hamsey Junction, for the Uckfield and (now) Bluebell lines. This also had a signal box.

Beyond this is Lewes (where the link line joins the Brighton to Eastbourne line), and then Southerham Junction, where the Seaford branch leaves the Eastbourne line, both already

unusual for three pretty platform shelters to survive on the same line (the others being at Plumpton and Berwick).

The original goods shed is behind the down platform. Despite closing in 1961, it continues in covered in Volume 1. Thus this history now continues the route on the Seaford branch, south of Southerham. From this point it passes over Glynde Reach, once navigable, and the site of Asheham Cement Works, which originally had a siding serving it. An overhead cableway passed from the works to a wharf on the River Ouse. Both were closed by 1971.

iv) Southease and Rodmell
The level crossing and signal box here predated the halt. The box was called Iford Crossing before being closed in 1960, while Southease and Rodmell Halt was opened on 1st September 1906. The crossing separated the platforms from the box. The platforms may have been moved from over the level crossing when the Southern Railway then replaced the wooden platforms with prefabricated ones.

Southease, September 2002. This is all that is now here. Photo: Paul O'Callaghan

Southease and Rodmell Halt, showing the crossing keeper's cottage and signal box, 6th June 1972. Photo: John Scrace

v) North of Newhaven Town
To clarify the history of the various sidings and short freight branches running off from the Seaford branch in Newhaven, we will examine the history of each of them as they come up along the route.

A siding originally left the branch on the east side to serve Sussex Portland Cement Works, while in 1891 sidings opened to serve the North Quay. More were then laid on the east side of the Seaford branch to serve ammunition trains and other requirements during World War One, as troops and supplies went to and from France using Newhaven, as it was out of range of the Germans. The North Quay sidings were overseen by Newhaven North signal box, which closed in January 1934. The goods shed stood north of the level crossing at Newhaven Town (where the road flyover now is), before the West Quay branch opened (see Chapter 3).

vi) Newhaven Town/Railway Wharf Line

Returning to Newhaven Town level crossing, the Seaford line passes the Newhaven B signal box on its east side, before the tracks go over the level crossing. Beyond the crossing, whilst the Seaford branch enters Newhaven Town station, a further branch once turned off to the right to serve the engine shed and railway wharf. The shed opened in 1887, but was reduced in status to a sub-shed of Brighton in September 1955 before final closure on 9th September 1963. A private business then took over the site. The shed had a 60 ft turntable from 1917 until 1962. The tracks pass along the wharf (east river embankment) and are joined by sidings from the Seaford branch just south of Newhaven Town Station, before ending beside Harbour Station.

Returning to Newhaven Town, the Seaford branch passes through the standard two-platform station, which still retains the Sussex flint building on the up platform, although the down platform has now lost its weatherboarded shelter.

ABOVE: Newhaven Town Station in 2002. Photo: Paul O'Callaghan
BELOW: Locos 4-4-2 32424, 50154 and 32640 at Newhaven shed, 1950s.
Photo: Hugh Davies/Photos From The Fifties

vii) Newhaven Harbour

After a quarter of a mile, past the sidings to the wharf line on the right, Newhaven Harbour Station is reached. Like Newhaven Town, the station is a simple two-platform affair. The long brick station building is on the down platform but is no longer used as such. It was once home to a model railway society, but now looks run down. Today a curved roof platform shelter is in front of the building. To the west of the station were the sidings and tracks from the engine shed and railway wharf described earlier. The *London & Paris Hotel* once stood next to the station from 1848, on the west side, south of the up platform. A customs house existed

Loco at Newhaven docks, 19th June 1963. Photo: R K Blencowe

Loco 10387 at Newhaven Harbour Station, with the 11.56 Lewes to Seaford train, 11th October 1933. Photo: H C Casserley

beyond here. Tracks from the wharf line lay on either side of it, ending just before the customs watch house. Originally this area south of Harbour Station (in fact, the whole area south of Mill Creek) was known as the 'Salts'.

When the LBSCR carried out their improvement works in the late 1870s, they blocked up Mill Creek mouth (which can be seen on the right from a train leaving Newhaven towards Seaford) where it flowed out into the Ouse, adding a third platform to Harbour Station. Confusingly, this additional platform and its station building were separate to the original, but in use as the Harbour Station. The third platform then became what was Newhaven Marine Station (which we will call it throughout, so as to avoid confusion), a separate station used only by boat trains from London. However, this was mothballed in the first few years of the 21st century. To clarify: if looking south from Newhaven Harbour Station footbridge when this entire layout existed, one would have seen the Seaford branch curving left,

then from that the tracks into Newhaven Marine Station platform, and then tracks going directly ahead, passing between Marine Station and the hotel.

Newhaven Marine Station consisted of a weatherboarded, finely designed building upon a platform serving one track. Immediately beyond the track was a second platform serving both that and another track on its east side, with further ones after it. The wooden platform canopy stretched from the station building across the first tracks and onto the second platform. This building and canopy is the

H2 Class loco (working RCTS Special) on the turntable at Newhaven, 1950s. Photo: Norman Simmons, supplied by Photos From The Fifties/Hugh Davies

Newhaven Marine Station, September 2002, clearly showing its unusually extended canopy. Photo: Paul O'Callaghan

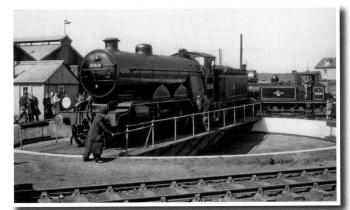

A train from Seaford approaches, the tracks ahead going into Newhaven Marine Station, with the signal box on the right. Photo: Paul O'Callaghan

which passed in front of Marine Station. From here the track became the East Quay branch or, as some people call it, the Beach Tramway, curving left to run along the top of the beach. As it did so it was joined by a siding from the lighthouse at the east mouth of the Ouse. East Quay branch was slowly extended over the years, generally for wagons to be filled with shingle, which would be hauled around Newhaven to help with the construction of the breakwater. In fact, by 1940 the line may have reached the

Loco 32479 shunting on the docks line, with Newhaven Town Station on the left, 19th June 1963. Photo: R K Blencowe

structure most often shown in pictures of the Newhaven branch. Interestingly, the Marine Station track area was not electrified until 16th July 1947, so Marine trains from London remained steam-hauled after the Seaford branch itself had been electrified. During World War Two, the hotel, having been taken over by the Navy, was bombed and subsequently pulled down in 1956.

Beyond this, before the tracks behind it ended at the sea edge, connecting rails went from them to join with tracks

Tracks from the Newhaven East Quay branch, south of Tide Mills, still surviving in September 2002. Photo: Paul O'Callaghan

(now preserved on the Bluebell Railway), could pass over this section. In 1975, this last worn-down section of track was surfaced as a road to be used for access to a yacht club. During the 1960s, a further branch was laid to serve the construction of the Royal Sovereign lightship station.

To create more room for sidings at Newhaven Town, more of Mill Creek and its saltings were eventually filled in. To help with this, sidings were laid north of the East Quay branch (before Tide Mills) to handle wagons of spoil for the infilling.

Loco 32636 at Newhaven, 18th August 1951. Photo: R M Casserley

halfway point between the ruined village of Tide Mills on the north side and the *Buckle Inn* at modern Bishopstone. This may be why some bits of track work can still be found along this coastline (although some parts could be due to the 80 yards of narrow gauge track set into a large concrete base for a sea plane base around 1930). Due to the worn track of the East Quay branch between the said halfway point and Tide Mills, a sign was erected in 1956 warning that only locomotives of certain classes, like Fenchurch

viii) Tide Mills and First Bishopstone Station

Returning to Newhaven Harbour Station, the Seaford branch curves left out of the station, leaving the Marine Station tracks to go off to the right. The line, single track from hereon, passes the remains of Mill Creek on the right. On approaching Tide Mills village, before the site of the first Bishopstone Station, which opened on 1st June 1864, a siding turned off southwards to run through the main street of the village to the mill itself. In 1883 the mill stopped grinding and by 1901 the street section of the siding had been lifted. The station had two platforms, but was reduced

Postcard looking across Newhaven Harbour towards Seaford Bay, 1950s. Rails can be seen far right, while buildings still stand at Tide Mills (distance, left).

Bridge near the Buckle Inn*, Bishopstone, 2002. Photo: Paul O'Callaghan*

in status to a halt in 1922. The village became little used after the mill closed, and the station ceased operation on 26th September 1938 when a new Bishopstone Station (the present one) opened. However, the old station briefly reopened as Bishopstone Beach on 1st April 1939, to serve a retirement home, before closing for good on 1st January 1942. Both platforms survive, and retained their platform shelters until at least 1947.

iix) Bishopstone Second Station (Current)

After passing over an arched bridge at the *Buckle Inn*, the line enters the new Bishopstone Station, a building of art

ABOVE: Bishopstone Station's distinctive booking hall roof. BELOW: The station itself, August 2002, with gun turret upper windows, fitted during World War Two! Photos: Paul O'Callaghan

deco design which opened on 26th September 1938. Its platforms lie in a cutting and there is one shelter on the up platform, although today only this side retains a track. A roofed footbridge links the platforms to the Southern Railway-designed station building on the north side. Fascinatingly, in 1940 small 'pill boxes' (gun emplacements) were added around its roof for use in case of a German invasion. The station was constructed to serve an expected residential development, but building was delayed by the war. In 2002, staff were removed from the station.

ix) Seaford

Beyond Bishopstone it is only a short straight run to Seaford Station. This originally consisted of just one platform and the two-storey, three-bay station building, with tracks in front of the platform merging on a sector plate, a sort of turntable. A roadside canopy was added to the front later. The station is painted in stucco cement, with slate roofs. The two-storey building also has two single-storey wings. It is of Italianate style with 2-3-2 windows in the two-storey part, with three bay windows and two arched-headed sashes and an off-centre arched door. The wings have two ground and two first-floor segmental-headed windows, repeated in the three centre bays. All four have pane plate glass sashes. (Other interesting architectural features include a canopy

ABOVE: Seaford Station, 21st May 1975. Photo: John Scrace BELOW: The roadside entrance to Seaford Station, 2008. Photo: Paul O'Callaghan

on brackets with a balance to three centre bays, a modillion bracket cornice, and returned hipped gables with two stuccoed stalks, while the single-storey wings have straight headed and segmental headed openings, modillion cornices and a single tall stalk to both wings).

On the south side of the tracks was the first goods shed (demolished during or after 1986). From 1892, a second goods shed, a siding, turntable and coal depot were erected on the north side of the station. The goods yard shut in 1962. When the line was doubled, Seaford Station gained a bay platform, the second track terminating on the other side of its existing platform against the station building. After the line was later singled again, the bay platform track and a siding next to the main platform track lingered on. Unusually, the roadside canopy still survives. The platform canopy consists of nine bays with cast-iron columns displaying simplified stiff leaf-style capitals branching into stanchions with roundels in spandrels, and the windows are round-headed. It was statutory listed on 26th March 1987 due to its being an unaltered and still complete example of a terminus station building retaining its canopies, according to English Heritage.

Like Dungeness and Winchelsea Beach, old railway carriages used to be stored around Seaford during both the 19th and 20th centuries.

Chapter 3: Newhaven West Quay Branch

Background

When old pictures of a railway at Newhaven appear, it is usually of the West Quay branch line. In the 1970s, ferries from here to France were at the mercy of the tide (low tide, for instance, prevented big ships from entering Newhaven), thus affecting the number of trains to Newhaven Harbour. In 1876 the LBSCR obtained the legal rights to buy the Harbour Board, but did not use them. Instead it formed its own company, the Newhaven Harbour Company, in 1878. The Harbour Board badgered the government to use public money to improve the facilities (e.g. lowering the river bed) so that bigger boats could enter at low tide. The government refused, so the LBSCR, using its new company, funded the improvement works itself. As part of this, the LBSCR needed to create a long breakwater (also known as a 'mole') to the west of the river mouth. (Its construction was covered in Chapter 2.)

The Route

To create the breakwater, a West Quay railway was required. It began just before the Seaford branch passed over the level crossing at Newhaven Town Station. The Quay branch passed over the River Ouse by way of an iron swing bridge

ABOVE: Old postcard (undated) showing the West Quay, with the railway on the breakwater to the right. BELOW: Loco 37678 by the West Quay lighthouse, 27th July 1963. Photo: R C Riley

Loco 32636 on the West Quay, 12th July 1950. Photo: R C Riley

On the bridge, a flagman walked ahead of the train ringing a bell, as the train passed along its rails in the road. This practice ceased during World War Two (presumably so that people didn't mistake it as a bell indicating invasion) and was not restored afterwards. Once over the bridge, the West Quay branch ran along the west bank of the Ouse, passing around the Sleepers Hole lagoon and then around the edge of the foot of the west cliff (where, until 1925, a short siding went to the corner of the river and sea to serve the lighthouse). From there it passed the *Hope Inn*, to run

Loco 32678 on the West Quay branch swing bridge at Newhaven, with rails embedded into the road, 27th July 1963. Photo: R C Riley

(replacing a previous wooden construction), constructed and designed by LBSCR engineers 13 years before the branch was laid over the bridge, sharing it in later years with motor cars. It was manually operated by eight men. When the mechanism was opened, gas pipes had to be blocked off, as they passed through the infrastructure. In 1976, the swing bridge was abolished, with a new one (the current version) being built just to the north. The old abutments can still be seen, while the main road was realigned to go over the new bridge.

Loco 32678 leaving Newhaven swing bridge, 27th July 1963. Photo: R C Riley

Sleepers Hole on the north side, the branch was crossed by standard gauge tracks belonging to Meeching Quarry (owned by the Earl of Sheffield), connecting it to the river wharf, with a full track connection made to the West Quay branch after 1898. The quarry opened in 1880 and closed in 1939, having changed ownership to Colgate & Gray in 1882. Horses hauled wagons here, full of ballast and whiting chalk, and ice was also shipped in from Germany. The horses would often pass the nearby *Sheffield Arms* hotel.

The remains of the old swing bridge abutment on the east bank of the Ouse, September 2002. Photo: Paul O'Callaghan

along the seafront, continuing on to the breakwater once it was finished. At the sea end, before turning to go onto the breakwater, there were sidings for wagons to be filled with ballast. The West Quay line also served an oil depot (used for an oil-powered ferry) from 1928 until 1958-59, as well as a tarpaulin and rope works in warehouses which closed on 2nd August 1963. On one occasion, the track had to be re-laid beyond the *Hope Inn* due to storm damage.

Close to where the West Quay branch passed around

ABOVE: Loco 32678 at Breakwater Siding, Newhaven, 27th July 1963.
BELOW: The same loco at West Quay sidings. Photos: R C Riley

With the loss of business when the rope works ended, the West Quay line closed just days later on 10th August 1963, the last train going to collect wagons hauled by Terrier 32678. By 1963, the track on the breakwater was in any case no longer safe for trains to go onto.

Chapter 4: Eastbourne's Other Railway - The Crumbles Branch

Background

Beyond the main Eastbourne line itself (explored in Volume 1), there was another railway that was almost as important to the development of the town: The Crumbles Branch.

The Crumbles is a massive bank of shingle, much of which has today been eaten away to create Eastbourne Marina. Back in the 19th century, after negotiations with the Crumbles land owner, the Duke of Devonshire, in 1847 and 1862, the Crumbles branch line - sometimes referred to as the 'Gas Works & Ballast Hole Single Line', and also as 'Down Siding' - was constructed in 1862 and ran to a length of almost three and a half miles. It was laid by the London, Brighton & South Coast Railway company, which agreed to pay one penny for every yard of shingle, but

At the end of the Crumbles branch, showing the 'Herd's Tower', 1930s. Photo: Bob Cookson collection

branch; he needed the shingle for a housing development in Eastbourne. The stones would be hauled down the branch from the Crumbles to Eastbourne, and then on a track into the Duke's estate yard (which was beside the Upper Avenue/ Cavendish Road bridge over the railway, on the east side).

Another use for the Crumbles branch was for picturesque official photographs of trains, and for hauling fertiliser to local farms. The Southern Railway (the successor to LBSCR) ceased using shingle from the Crumbles, so the branch was closed east of the A259, from its intersection

E2 tank loco No. 100 at the Crumbles branch's ballast pit, 1920s. Photo: R C Riley (Bob Cookson collection)

using only the minimal amount of 48,000 tons a year. The purpose of the shingle was for use as track ballast (the stones beneath railway tracks), and the branch enabled wagons of shingle to be hauled up and down from the Crumbles by steam locomotives. It was also unfenced, although a guard travelled on the loco for the task of opening and closing crossing gates.

The Duke of Devonshire, despite charging the LBSCR for use of the Crumbles, also had his own interest in using the

*The Eastbourne gasworks loco No. 1, 'Mary', date unknown.
Photo: Bob Cookson collection*

gasworks (opened in 1870), which had its own two steam locomotives, 'Mary' and 'Anne' (built by the Avonside company in 1909), to work its own sidings, which ran off from the Crumbles line. When the sidings were closed in 1967, the locomotives were offered for sale in *Railway Magazine*. Sadly, no takers were forthcoming, so the locomotives were cut up for scrap. In 1960 the locomotives for the Crumbles were replaced by a 204hp 0-6-0DM shunter from Brighton. In June 1962, a steam locomotive

View from Seaside Road, looking north behind the crossing keeper's house. The trolleys were for track demolition. Photo: Sid Nash (Bob Cookson collection)

with the road at a level crossing, where a crossing keeper's house (built with Kentish weather/clapboarding and with a chimney upon a slate roof) once stood. Until 1932, train drivers passing this point would whistle to alert the public that a train was coming. The drivers were also known to give local boys a lift to school. Today this site is the location of the roundabout beside Tesco's superstore and a dentist.

The Crumbles branch was retained west of the A259 Seaside Road to serve private businesses along the route, some of which had their own sidings. One business was the reappeared briefly in the form of Terrier (Stroudley) A1X Class 0-60T No. 32636 when a diesel wasn't available, and a larger locomotive type arrived in 1965.

There was also a half-mile branch leaving the Crumbles line, turning off to the south before the gasworks. This served the electricity works from 1926, with increasing coal trains on the line to power it, and ended in November 1966, with the works finally closing in February 1967.

The Crumbles branch also closed in 1967 (the last consignment of coal for the gasworks arriving on 28th March). Until 7th July 1968, railway journeys continued on the line using cable wagons (as power supply cables were being renewed), but in summer 1970 the track was finally lifted.

Goods train on the Crumbles branch, date unknown.
Photo: Bob Cookson collection

The Route

i) Roselands (Waterworks, Gasworks, Electricity Works Junction)

The Crumbles line was operated on the only-one-engine-in-steam method, as there was no signalling on the branch. However, a train staff system was used until 1946. On the return journey, until 1935 the locomotive would whistle at the coal yard in Eastbourne, which would then alert the signal box at Eastbourne (!), but thereafter a phone was added at the signal so that the loco crew could contact the

box directly. The phone survived through the British Rail years, but the signal was removed. Retracing the route back up from Eastbourne to Whitley Road railway bridge and the waterworks, the Crumbles track veered away to the right as the Eastbourne branch bent left. The Crumbles route originally ran around the north side of the Roselands area, but since the line closed the Roselands estate has spread northwards across the route of the old branch. The Crumbles line did eventually head north eastwards, passing across what is now Ringwood Road, and then between what is now Astaire Avenue and Bridgemere Road (where the railway bridge over a stream continued to be used after being converted to a footpath), before heading around the rear of Northbourne Road and passing along the south side of the gasworks, before reaching Seaside Road level crossing.

After the gasworks, the Crumbles branch arrived at Lewis Gasson's timber yard, which was on the north side. Its siding was also used by another timber company, Messrs. White & Co.

Train passing Llewellyn's Yard on the Crumbles branch, date unknown. Photo: J J Smith (Bob Cookson collection)

ii) Seaside Road Level Crossing

Until 1932, trains continued to rumble across Seaside Road (the A259) where on the east side of the road stood a weatherboarded crossing keeper's house. Today a large roundabout has been constructed here, with a large Tesco on the west side, its car park covering the former track bed of the branch. The rails in the road and beyond, on the east side, were left to rust until 1950.

iii) Queens Crescent and Wallis Avenue

Beyond Seaside Road, the Crumbles branch headed north-eastwards after 40 yards, passing the British Petroleum Company's siding. Then it ran behind the east side of Queens Crescent and over Wallis Avenue, heading out across the Crumbles itself. Looking at old maps and comparing the Pevensey Bay Road and coastline, one can make a rough guess that beyond Wallis Avenue the Crumbles branch would have passed through the centre of what is now the Marina, then across where the northern Marina harbour is now located, ending close to Martello Tower 64 (Herd's Tower, which is still standing).

iv) The Crumbles

As is clear on visual inspection, the area from Cooden Beach is very flat reclaimed land. In fact, from Cooden Beach all the way to Eastbourne (south of the Redoubt - see below), 2000 years ago this whole area was a bay when the Romans arrived, and it stretched inland as far as Hailsham. The long shore drift of the sea gathered up pebbles and rocks along the seabed from Beachy Head and began to accumulate along the front of the bay. Over 200 years, this accumulation linked islets to form a shingle bank, eventually separating the bay from the sea and creating a lagoon, which began to silt up. A harbour at Pevensey still managed to exist as a limb (as Winchelsea was to Rye) of the Cinque Port of Northeye, at the north side of the lagoon.

This bank of stones between Eastbourne and Pevensey would become known as 'The Crumbles', which existed as a large wildlife area until it was dug out and built on to make Eastbourne Marina in the early 1990s (leaving only patches of its original state). The Crumbles was two miles in length and essentially fully formed by the 11th century (when the Normans invaded), although Langney Point didn't appear until later (it was certainly there by 1736). Since then The Crumbles has reduced in width, as the sea has eroded the shingle (look out, Marina!). Wooden groynes have been installed to protect The Crumbles, and barges have to bring in fresh shingle to replenish the banks every winter.

The term 'Crumble' comes from the old English word *Cuma*, meaning the bank is a crumb of stony ground. Most

Overgrown track at the Crumbles branch, 3rd October 1948. Photo: J J Smith (Bob Cookson collection)

of the Crumbles coastline has now been invaded by the Marina, and development still goes on today. The flowers and plants of The Crumbles have been much reduced, undermining the insect and animal population (such as lizards). The lake in Prince's Park, where men meet up to play with remote-controlled boats, was originally The Crumbles' pond, dating back to at least the 13th century.

v) Electricity Works Branch

Returning to the electricity works junction, this is where the short branch to Eastbourne's works swing off to the

Loco E4 2406 crosses St Philips Avenue on the electricity works branch, 1949.
Photo: S C Nash (Bob Cookson collection)

right, heading south-eastward across Astaire Avenue, then between Hunlocke and Harding Avenues and across St Philips Avenue, before swinging left to head north-easterly across Roselands Avenue to the works on the north-west side of Windermere Crescent.

Chapter 5: The Rye Harbour Branch and Narrow Gauge Railways

Background

As part of the construction of the Ashford to Hastings line, the SER opted to build a freight-only branch along the south side of the River Rother to its mouth. The junction with the Rye line would face Hastings. It gave £10,000 to the Admiralty by March 1846 (having only opted to do so on 18th September 1845).

Meanwhile, Robert Stephenson had advised that the branch be 1.75 miles long, and an Act was obtained on 18th June 1846. Wythes built the branch (along with other work on the Ashford-Hastings route) for £131,000. After Ashford-Hastings opened, Rye residents complained about the lack of progress with the Harbour branch, so Wythes was told to finish it in March 1851, but a second Act was required so that legal powers could be obtained to build a 'tramroad' at The Strand. Complaints continued to come in during February and March 1852 due to the slow developments, the branch being nowhere near finished even by March 1853. However, in March 1854, the SER became interested in running a ferry service to Normandy from Rye Harbour, so the branch was finally rushed to completion that month, and duly opened – but the ferry service never started! A new jetty was eventually constructed for freight/private business in 1903 for £2,200, replacing its rotted and silted up predecessor.

There were various private sidings running off the branch into businesses, with some passing over the main road to the harbour. These included chemical works (its siding's tracks still embedded beside the main road it used to cross in 1991), a tar vat, tile and brick works, and stone works.

The 2 ft narrow gauge railways of Simpson (Rye Harbour) Ltd (for shingle movement) and Pett Level Tramway (for

Disused factory siding near Rye Harbour, 1991. Photo: Paul O'Callaghan

repairing beach defences), when connected by 1937, in effect formed a little coastal railway of their own. The line started from the Rye Harbour branch and then went between a school and the Church of the Holy Spirit (it was originally laid to pass the church on the east side of it), before running along the coast to Cliff End for a length of five miles, giving Winchelsea Beach its own line. Pett Level Tramway closed in 1946.

The Harbour branch ended on a pier to the east of the *William the Conqueror* public house, beside the Rother river. The Golf Links station (which still stands) of the Rye & Camber Tramway overlooked the Harbour branch from across the Rother. In 1895, it was proposed to expand Rye harbour and construct a 'double loop line', but this idea was shelved. The pier was eventually declared unsafe, so another buffer stop was erected on the Harbour branch at the land end of the pier. Finally, on 29th January 1960, the branch was closed.

Rye Harbour's Private Railways

Along the Rye Harbour branch and its main road, there are various industrial works, some of these (and earlier works) having had sidings from the branch itself and nearby narrow gauge railways:

i) A siding from the branch lay between the Rye-Winchelsea road and the River Brede, on the north side (serving John Carter's).

ii) Further down the Harbour branch, another siding left it, crossing the main road and going up to the River Rother. This served the Rye Chemical & Manufacturing Company (or South Eastern Tar Distilleries, later ABCO Petroleum). It was a dual gauge railway, with one of 2 ft. In the 1960s, a Ruston Hornby locomotive (diesel) was used. Some of the track in the entrance to the works, beside the main road, survived into 1991 (see photo, previous page). This works later acquired the steam crane from the Admiralty pier.

iii) The next significant narrow gauge system used a 'Simpson's track', which began at an interchange platform with the Harbour branch, about five minutes walk north of the church. It left the branch at the platform, before crossing the main road to go south, where a track left a siding on its right, on its west side to a stone works. As it curved south east to go behind the church on its left, a few tracks carried on beside the road, passing through a structure where one swung left behind the church lychgate, across the main road, over the Harbour branch and up to the River Rother.

The main track of the narrow gauge system (passing behind the churchyard) curved to go south, splitting in two, with the right (west) track becoming a tramway while the left (east) track joined with a track from sidings in the stone works to the north east of the church.

Further History

The aforementioned layout was that established by 1929. However, in 1937 it was greatly simplified: the track from the river was reduced in length, ending on the south side of the Harbour branch (by curving to the left to run alongside it for a short way). The track from the Harbour branch then went directly south, along the east side of the church, passing between this and the school before rejoining the old route to the stone works and tramway. The previous layout behind and to the west of the church, and the platform, had all been removed by 1937.

Following a storm in 1926, which breached local flood defences, by 1934 the Rother & Jury Gut Catchment Board had found enough money to fix them. To help with the repairs, a 2 ft gauge railway was laid from Cliff End up to Winchelsea Lifeboat Station in 1936, and the year after it was linked with a Simpson's narrow gauge railway system 220 yards from the beach, beside a Simpson's gravel pit. Shingle was carried by these trains to fill a new box-wall (two wooden walls 13 feet apart) with horizontal planks holding both sides together. There was space between the planks to put the shingle through to fill up the box-wall, which stretched from Cliff End to the lifeboat station. One can imagine materials being brought in down the Harbour branch to repair the sea defences, then being transferred to the 2 ft gauge train on the Simpson's system beside it, which would then traverse that to go onto the flood defence repair line to reach Winchelsea Beach and Cliff End (Fairlight).

In 1946, with all repairs complete, the new tracks (to Winchelsea Beach and Cliff End) were lifted. At least two photographs of this defence repair line exist in Hastings Library (see picture, page 78). However, in 1947 a superior sea wall was begun, and finished in 1952.

Other Nearby Lines

At the 1872 end of the Harbour branch (before it was extended onto the pier), a turntable connected it with a line that passed behind the *William the Conqueror* public house and Coast Blockade House, across the main road and then straight down into a concrete works, south of Rye harbour village. A siding from the works went in front of the said buildings to Admiralty Quay, thus giving it direct access to both the Harbour branch and the Rother (where Admiralty Pier was later built). The works were undertaken in 1859

for Messrs. Lee & Sons, who were creating concrete blocks to help build Dover harbour. The embankment part of this line survives. A further line led to the beach, so that shingle could be moved to the works.

A man called Tom Firrell operated one of the narrow gauge railways, which hauled skip wagons holding blue boulders, which were then taken (presumably by a Harbour branch train) to glazing establishments around Britain. It also hauled trains of shingle to a harbour business for crushing. Mr Firrell also repaired the locomotives (in fact he was once

Siding at Rye Harbour, 1950s. Photo: Lens of Sutton collection

also a witness to the lifeboat sinking, sending a colleague in a train to speed down to the Coast Guard to alert them).

This information on Tom Firrell is based on accounts in *Bygone Rye Harbour*, reproduced here with the kind permission of Jo Kirkham, its editor.

Chapter 6: The Dungeness/ New Romney Branch Line

General History

The first proposal for a branch to New Romney from Appledore was made in 1866 and did receive authorisation, but no further action was taken.

Then, in 1873, the Rye & Dungeness & Pier Company was established as part of a plan to set up a harbour at Dungeness, with a line ten and three quarter miles long. Dungeness beach runs steeply down into the sea; just 30 ft from the coast the depth reaches five fathoms before deepening quickly to fifteen. Thus Dungeness, as well as being the southernmost point of Kent, is the closest to land that large ships can get when sailing up the English Channel, making it an ideal location for a harbour.

The line was authorised on 5th August 1873, but the Pier Company did not build anything either. However,

Loco at Dungeness, 1930. Photo: Lens of Sutton collection

legal powers were transferred to the SER in 1875, after its chairman, Sir Edward Watkin, voiced concern that the scheme could be taken over by a rival company. Watkin chaired the Metropolitan Railway and what was to become the Great Central Railway, and he was also local MP for the Folkestone area. His dream was to run trains from Manchester to France, and was campaigning to create a tunnel under the English Channel. In case this didn't succeed, he had a back up plan: to turn Dungeness into a port. As this was just 70 miles from London, with a steam boat service from Dungeness to Le Treport, passengers would only be 114 miles from Paris by train. Thus a fast transport route from London to Paris would be established.

Construction and Opening

The Lydd Railway Company was eventually formed to build and own the new line, but it was in reality a puppet company of the SER. Edward Watkin's son Alfred was the chairman of the Lydd Company. The engineer was the SER's Francis Brady, and the contractor was Thomas Walker. It was built using old recycled track from the Hastings line. A capital of £175,000 was sanctioned for the branch, which began in the parish of Kenardington near to the platforms of Appledore, and ended approximately 330 yards north of the (now disused) lighthouse. It was to cost less than £2,000 per mile.

Due to the flatness of the land, the Lydd Company line was quickly constructed and opened on 7th December 1881 (the day after its ceremonial opening), running as far as Lydd station for passengers and goods trains, although only goods trains went beyond to Dungeness. The opening day was full of festivities, as a special train arrived filled with Lydd and SER directors, led by Edward Watkin. It was a foggy day to begin with, but the sun soon broke through. Local officials greeted the directors with a military band, before the party drove in a horse-drawn carriage to Lydd Town Hall for a meal, where they raised toasts, joked, and

waxed lyrical about the future of the harbour. (A detailed account of the two opening days can be found in Peter A Harding's *New Romney Branch Line*).

The line to Dungeness opened to passengers on 1st April 1883, with, again, Edward Watkin leading the gentry and directors, arriving on another special train. They had lunch in the lighthouse, at which some of the party discussed how the sea movement on the shingle could be harnessed to speed up the creation of the Harbour.

Dungeness lighthouse, with the line running directly alongside, 1930.
Photo: Lens of Sutton collection

On 24th July 1882, the Lydd Company was given consent to build a branch from its railway to New Romney, which was to be three miles and 24 yards long, terminating at Gun Lane. Francis Brady was engineer. It was expected to cost £10,700. In addition, this 1882 authorisation gave permission to the Lydd company to extend from Appledore up to Headcorn via Tenterden. On 25th January 1883, further powers were sought to construct a line from Headcorn to Loose (near Maidstone and the Medway Valley line), which would have created a new main line to Dungeness. In 1891, Alfred Watkin began to transfer the legal rights to the SER (which bought 1,000 acres at Dungeness) and another SER puppet company, the Cranbrook & Paddock Wood Railway Company. On 21st June 1892, the powers for the extensions to Headcorn and Loose were officially transferred to the SER.

On 19th June 1884, the New Romney Branch opened for business, the ceremonial opening day occurring the day before, with Edward Watkin and his directors arrived by official train yet again, and this time waxing lyrical at the New Romney Town Hall, having been greeted by the Mayor at the flag-covered station. Fireworks concluded the evening. However, for all the celebration, the Board of Trade report on the line criticised the lack of gates at level crossings, and in January 1895 the SER absorbed the puppet Lydd company. The extensions to Headcorn and Loose were never constructed, due to the expensive work needed to run them through steep hillsides.

Further proposals were put forward for a South Kent Railway in 1896; a Cinque Ports Light Railway (a 3 ft, 6 inch gauge electric line from Hastings to Ramsgate) in 1899; an extension of the new Rother Valley Railway at Tenterden to Appledore in 1902; and an extension to Hythe. But none of these were built either.

From 1899 until the First World War, the South Eastern & Chatham Railway Managing Committee (set up by the SER and its rival to operate their lines) dabbled with ideas for extending the New Romney branch, first as an expansion of a tramway from the one they owned from Hythe to Sandgate, then as a light railway in 1900 (which should have been finished by 1903). In 1904, the SECR wanted to move the route of the proposed light railway line to Hythe, and then began to operate a bus service between Hythe and New Romney in 1914. Thus a passenger from Appledore to Hythe could travel by the SECR transport via New Romney, even if part of the journey was by bus.

The First World War stopped this. During it, Zeppelins used the New Romney railway tracks as a guide to reach London to bomb it, although on one occasion the intruder got lost and was later shot down, killing all aboard.

The Littlestone-on-Sea train at New Romney Station, 1950s. Note the heavily overgrown up platform in the foreground. Photo: Norman Simmons

After the Southern Railway absorbed the SER in 1923, a lot of holiday makers used the branch to reach the coast, so the SR opted to move the New Romney branch line between Romney Junction (where the New Romney branch left the Dungeness branch) and New Romney itself, closer to the coastline. Two new stations were opened; Lydd-on-Sea and Greatstone-on-Sea. By this time the Romney, Hythe & Dymchurch Railway (RHDR) had opened (in 1927 from Hythe to New Romney, and to Dungeness two years later). The short stretch of line between SR's Romney Junction

and Dungeness closed to passengers on the day the new section of line opened on 4th July 1937, as Lydd-on-Sea now served Dungeness and Lydd became Lydd Town.

During the Second World War, train services were reduced, and an armoured train operated on the branch (as described in Volume 1). On one occasion a Luftwaffe pilot decided to attack a train near Swamp Crossing, but came down too low, hitting the locomotive's (No. 2365) dome, and crashing into a field. The pilot, it is claimed, was thrown from his plane into a ditch where he drowned. The loco crew survived and the engine was repaired.

In 1948, the Southern Railway was absorbed into British Railways (British Rail from the 1960s) and the Romney Junction to Dungeness section of line was closed in May 1953. Dr Richard Beeching, chairman of BR in 1963, listed the New Romney Branch for closure as part of his plan to close two-thirds of Britain's railways. The end came on 6th March 1967 (completely for the New Romney-Romney Junction section of line, and just to passenger services on the Appledore–Romney Junction section), after being delayed due to the need for a replacement bus service. It was the Transport Minister, the late Barbara Castle, who implemented the closure (some alleged for political reasons, as the area was not held by Labour). Lydd Station continued to have goods trains until 4th October 1971.

Until 1980, a local firm had sidings at Lydd station for aggregates traffic. Since then, only nuclear waste trains from Dungeness power station have used the route, and the line has a speed restriction of 20 mph. In 1999, comedian Mark Thomas staged a stunt for his Channel 4 television show to highlight the need for extra security around these trains by presenting himself and others as a security team at Lydd Station, fully convincing the driver, before following the nuclear train in a helicopter.

There were calls in the 1970s and early 1980s to fully reopen the line. Indeed, Lydd Station could be saved by becoming a heritage railway museum for the South Eastern & Chatham Railway Preservation Society's collection of railway items. Being surrounded by neighbouring heritage railways would help the museum gain custom.

However, there are two further options: A London to Ashford service could be extended to Lydd (boosting Lydd in many ways), or a direct service to Ashford could be installed. Otherwise, railway preservationists could re-extend the line to Dungeness, maybe creating an interchange station with the RHDR's Dungeness station, and operate diesel-hauled electric slam-door trains (4CIG, 4BEP and 4CEP units) and a former slam-door DMU Marshlink unit along the branch when the nuclear waste service is not operating.

The Route

As Appledore Station is already covered in Volume 1, we will here begin the route after the junction, where the up and down tracks ran off from the Hastings line and merged into a single track.

i) Brookland

After passing four level crossings, which each had gatekeeper cottages, a train would enter Brookland Station. It had two 176 ft platforms, the down hosting the station building, and the up with a waiting shelter similar to that surviving

Brookland Station, 1910. Photo: Lens of Sutton collection

Brookland Station, 1991, now converted to cottages. Photo: Paul O'Callaghan

door trains, more than once managed to plough through level crossing gates which failed to open for the trains.

ii) Lydd

After passing under the only bridge across the line (the main road bridge at Lydd) and over the old level crossing, trains entered Lydd station. This consisted of two platforms of 270 ft. The station building stood on the up platform (with a water tower at the north end) and was gabled with canopies above both the platform and roadside entrance doorways (still there in 2007), while the down platform had

Loco at Lydd-on-Sea Halt, 1950s. Photo: Lens of Sutton collection

at Rye. In 1921, the signal box at the north end of the up platform, and the loop line (serving the down platform), were taken out of use and Brookland became a halt. At the south end was a small brick building for the gatekeeper, who also served as booking clerk, beside the level crossing over the A259 main road, while the station buildings survived as private homes.

Beyond Brookland, the line crossed more level crossings, where both steam engines and, in the 1960s, DMU slam

Lydd Town Station, 19th November 1966. Photo: R K Blencowe

Lydd, which was served by a long siding from the station goods yard. Inside the base were up to six miles of track, some of it brought from the Suakin & Berber railway in Sudan. In 1927 much of this track and the siding were removed. Also in the base was a 60 cm narrow gauge railway, the track work for which, in 1990, if laid end to end in a straight line, would have been 15 miles long! This ran with five Hunslet locomotives, a carriage for staff to use to renew the tracks, and Wickham trolleys, which carried moving targets to shoot at, going at 15 mph. However, by 2000 this track had been reduced to five miles in length.

Lydd Station crossing, looking towards Dungeness, 1991. Photo: Paul O'Callaghan

a wooden shelter, which remained until 1917. Behind the station building, separated from it by the station approach road, were the goods sidings, goods shed and cattle dock. The signal box was adapted to use the Tyler's Electric Operation System when Romney Junction box was closed. The stationmaster at Lydd eventually became responsible for the whole line. After its closure, the station building was used as a tyre centre between 1987-1991, although it now looks as if it is going to collapse!

In 1883, a military base was established to the south of

iii) Dungeness
Beyond Lydd, the branch crossed over shingle terrain, passing

ABOVE: Site of Dungeness Station, minus track, April 2007. A diesel-hauled RHDR train can be seen distant left. BELOW: The end of the line at Romney Junction, April 2007. Photos: Paul O'Callaghan

the site of the first SER Romney Junction and, after one and a quarter miles, the new SR Romney Junction (the current end of the branch where the gantry now is). Then, a siding went off to the ECGB power station. The station terminus at Dungeness consisted of a weatherboarded horizontal-planked single storey building on the south side of the only platform (the up side). The track had a run-round loop, which itself had the Admiralty siding going off from it south eastwards, while at the opposite end a track went off to the ballast sidings. Today, a mound of earth with the concrete base of the Gents' toilets upon it is all that remains of this station, with the trackbed distinguishable for a quarter of a mile back up towards Romney Junction, still exhibiting some poles beside it.

iv) Lydd-on-Sea and Greatstone-on-Sea

Returning to the SR Romney Junction, the New Romney Branch originally had a stop known as 'Lydd-on-Sea for Dungeness'. It boasted a single waiting shelter and a passing loop. The 552 ft platform was an island type, being located between the two tracks, and connected to the approach road (also created by the Southern Railway) by a footbridge. The loop and footbridge were removed in 1954, when both stations were reduced to halts, as little housing or holiday traffic had developed here.

Greatstone-on-Sea Halt, around 1960. Photo: Lens of Sutton collection

time, was little utilised and gradually became disused and overgrown. The 343 ft up platform had a gable-ended station building upon it, with a canopy and a further waiting shelter-type structure almost next to it, to the south. Behind the down platform was the goods yard, which featured a shed. To the south stood the water tower, while opposite that, across the tracks, was the signal box (closed by the

A location put into perspective! An RHDR narrow gauge loco waits, just south of its New Romney station (behind the camera), while a full-size eight-carriage train awaits to depart from its own New Romney Station. Photo: Norman Simmons (Supplied by Photos From The Fifties/Hugh Davies)

The line then ran parallel to the RHDR tracks to Greatstone-on-Sea. It served a holiday camp and was much like Lydd-on-Sea, but with only a 446 ft platform and no loop or footbridge. The station car park did escape closure.

v) New Romney

At this point the branch, four miles from Dungeness lighthouse, rejoined the old SER route from Romney Junction, before entering New Romney Station. The 251 ft down platform, which did have a waiting shelter for a

1950s). There were also coal wharves, a loading dock and standard railway staff buildings.

In 1927, the up and down tracks were extended (as a re-merged single track) at the north end, across the main road and into the Romney, Hythe & Dymchurch Railway's New Romney station, which opened that year. The station was directly adjacent and needed coal. When the RHDR was extended in 1929 to Dungeness, the miniature gauge tracks passed right behind the down platform of the SER station, demonstrating how close the stations were. Seven years after the New Romney Branch closed, the RHDR station was expanded to cover the site of the coal siding. Today, no trace remains of the SER station, the site having become an industrial estate.

vi) The Fish Railways

Before leaving the Dungeness area, mention needs to be made of the Fish Railways. Due to the problem of getting over the rounded pebbles of shingle at Dungeness, narrow gauge tracks were laid for moving loads of fish. In 2000, eight were supposed to still exist, but by April 2007 only one remained intact. Dungeness is also home to several old railway carriages which have been converted into homes, although even more can be seen at Winchelsea.

ABOVE: Rusting remains of a fish railway at Dungeness, built for hauling fish wagons across the beach, April 2007. BELOW: Old railway carriages at Dungeness, converted to homes, April 2007. Photos: Paul O'Callaghan

Rye Tramway Station, with its petrol locomotive, 11th April 1931. The A259 River Rother bridge can be seen far right. Photo: H C Casserley

PART 2: Tramways and Other Small Lines

Chapter 7: The Rye & Camber Tramway

Background

The Rye & Camber Tramway is one of the great lost narrow gauge railways of Britain, like the Lynton & Barnstaple, Welsh Highland, Glyn Valley and the Leek & Manifold. Hopefully it will at some point be reborn like all but the latter of these lines. Various articles and books have been published about the tramway, but there is not the room here to bring to life in words the atmosphere of its operation as successfully as Peter A Harding did in his 1988 flagship booklet. After reading this, aged 13, I wanted to run my own model line (with a second, more easterly, terminus based on Bromley North Station), inspired by its ramshackle buildings, using scale replicas of its Baggnell locomotives. It wasn't long before I wanted to reopen the actual line itself. The R&CT was used by both golfers and holidaymakers heading for Camber Sands, so although not physically connected to the main Ashford–Hastings line, it was certainly reliant on the latter railway for trade, making it a close satellite.

General History

The R&CT was not, in truth, strictly a tramway, but to all appearances a railway. However, it lacked signals and did not need a Parliamentary Act to sanction its construction as it was laid on private land. It used a 3 ft gauge, like the Isle of Man railway today. In 1894, the Rye Golf Club opened for business, west of Camber Sands. The Harbour Branch (described in Part 1) lacked a passenger service, so local businessmen, seeing an opportunity, decided to open a railway from Rye to a point on the north bank of the Rother, opposite Rye harbour village (which was on the south side). A ferry across the Rother linked the village to the tramway. Thus, golfers, villagers and fishermen could all be served by the new line.

The Rye & Camber Tramway Company Ltd was registered into existence on 6th August 1895, and the line was constructed for £2,300, although the company was never a member of the Railway Clearing House. The engineer was Holman F Stephens, who built the Cranbrook & Paddock Wood, Hundred of Manhood (Selsey Branch), Sheppey Light, and Kent & East Sussex railways, which is why their stations are so similar. The chairman was Cuthbert Hayles,

Golf Links Station, 12th July 1931. Photo: H C Casserley

bridge across the Rother, so the request was rejected. Two Baggnell locomotives, named Camber and Victoria (the former slightly smaller than the latter), operated the line.

Opening Day

On 13th July 1895, the Rye & Camber Tramway opened from Rye Tram Station to Camber Station, where the Mayoress of Rye declared the line open and she was handed flowers by a Miss Marion Vidler. Later, a ceremonial lunch, where plenty of toasts took place, was also attended by a Dr

Loco at Rye Tramway Station, 11th April 1931. Photo: H C Casserley

and the Manckeloe Brothers of Horsemonden were the contractors. The track would run for one and three quarter miles (one mile, 31 chains and 22 yards). Due to the cost of construction, which gobbled up most of the capital for the line, the stations and layout were kept simple, with the Rye and Camber stations being built of corrugated iron and wood. The local council had asked for the Rye terminus to be built closer to the town (beside the River Rother and A259 road, east of Rye), but this would have meant an expensive and Mrs A E Vidler, with about two dozen other people, including the Mayors of both Rye and Winchelsea, and the contractor. (By chance, my ex-TV production course tutor was a Richard Vidler of Sidcup, who was distantly related to the Vidlers of Rye.) It took two trains to convey all the passengers to the Camber terminus, where a game of golf was later played. 18,000 tickets were sold during the line's first six months. From 1901, the R&CT required a subsidy from the Rye Golf Club, but finances improved in 1906. In

Rye Tramway Station (with petrol locomotive, far left), 2nd July 1931. Photo: H C Casserley

R&CT Loco No. 1, 'Camber', at Rye, 11th April 1931. Photo: H C Casserley

June 1908 there were ten trains on Monday to Fridays, with twelve on Saturdays and seven on Sundays.

With the boost in finances, the company directors decided to extend the tramway to a new station, Camber Sands, to enable passengers to access one of the few sandy beaches in East Sussex. The extension cost £650 in debentures and opened on 13th July 1908. The original Camber Station was renamed Golf Links. The usual ceremonial opening lunch and toasts followed at the golf club (where a Major Vidler was present). In 1912 there were 13 trains on weekdays, with seven going through to Camber Sands.

In time, however, financial problems resurfaced and worsened. In 1925, a petrol locomotive was introduced to reduce costs, replacing the steam locomotive Victoria, which was sold for scrap. That same year the golf club stopped subsidising the tramway. During the 1920s and 1930s, the wealthy golf clubbers began to use cars, and so could drive themselves there. In addition, in 1927, a bus service began to serve Rye Harbour village, and in the 1930s another bus

Rye Tramway Station, with the petrol loco and sheds beyond it, 11th April 1931. Photo: H C Casserley

Camber Sands, 11th April 1931. Photo: H C Casserley

began serving Camber. The Southern Railway considered taking over the line, but the cost of converting the tramway gauge and bridging the Rother was deemed too expensive, so this proposal was not pursued.

A re-routing of the extension was opened on 6th April 1939, the new Camber Sands terminus being south-east of the old one so that shingle could be collected and put into wagons to be hauled back to Rye for selling. However, this realignment was short lived as World War Two broke out and the tramway was closed on 4th September 1939. The admiralty took over the Rye to Golf Links section of line, so that men and materials could be transported to build a 1,000ft jetty on the north bank of the Rother. Mears Brothers Ltd laid concrete around the track west of Golf Links station as part of the access plan for building the jetty. One military man had an idea for reducing the RHDR double track between Hythe and New Romney to one track, so that another could be laid from Dungeness to Camber, converting the R&CT track gauge and thereby enabling the armoured train on the RHDR to travel up and down the entire vulnerable coastline between Hythe and Rye (the vulnerability of the coast and/or the Martello Towers are further discussed elsewhere in these volumes). After the war, the amount of money required to repair the tramway for renewed use deterred the company directors from reviving it and the Rye Corporation bought the land. In the early 21st century, there were attempts to have the line reopened, but the golf club blocked it as they own the land east of Golf Links.

In fact, a tramway here might be far more successful today than it was originally. A line with a Park & Ride facility could ferry day trippers, golfers and Camber residents, with discounts for the golfers as an encouragement for the club to allow its construction. As the club is east of Golf Links station, the Golf Links to Rye line could be reopened at least. As with the Lynton & Barnstaple railway (and with similar plans at Glyn Valley), a replica could be built of the

ABOVE: Rye Tramway Station, 11th April 1931. Photo: H C Casserley
BELOW: The same site 60 years later, in 1991. Photo: Paul O'Callaghan

Golf Links, as seen from across the Rother at Rye Harbour, with the buffer at the end of the branch, 1950s. Photo: David Lawrence (Photos From the Fifties)

R&CT's locomotives, Camber and Victoria, and even the petrol locomotive. Getting one of these built and establishing a museum of the line might well help the tramway to be reopened, showing that the scheme's promoters are not merely dreamers. With a reopened line to Golf Links, the club might give in and allow it to run to Camber Sands once more. Or railway buffs could always buy the golf club to get the tramway back! It could all start with the formation of a Rye & Camber Tramway Trust. Who knows what might be achieved?

The Route

i) Rye Tramway Terminus

The site of the terminus was beside the Monkbretton Bridge, carrying the main A259 road across the Rother, just east of Rye. It had a short platform with a corrugated building on its north side. The building was not as wide as its roof, so on the platform side the roof sloped over, doubling as the canopy, held up by three posts at one end. There was a track to serve the platform, with a run-round loop for locomotives to bypass their own carriages and enable them to get to the front of the train. A locomotive shed stood at the west end of the platform track, which was doubled to take a second track from the loop in 1896. A lean-to structure was later added to the station, as were further sheds at the east end, passing slightly behind the station building. The station was demolished in 1947.

Beyond Rye, 900 yards along, the single track passed over Bridgewater Stream (the bridge now carried a pipe) to Northpoint Beach (now flooded but it can be got around), crossing over the 2 ft gauge tramway of Colebrooke's, which existed for collecting shingle. 1,300 yards along, the line passed Golf View House (later named Beechlands, and then Squatters Right), now demolished, where trains stopped if requested.

ABOVE: Golf Links Station, facing Rye, 12th July 1931. Photo: H C Casserley
BELOW: The same site, 1991, rails then still intact. Photo: Paul O'Callaghan

ii) Golf Links

Like the Rye terminus, this station building was narrower than its roof, which sloped over on the platform side, doubling as the canopy, again held with three posts, if slightly smaller overall. The building stood on a short brick and concrete platform (again like Rye) with a single track and run-round loop, which was removed when the line was extended to Camber Sands, but put back by the Admiralty with a siding running to a pier at its west end. Since its closure, the front of the station has been expanded across the platform, so the roof now covers an entire building (painted green in 2007), which is used today as a store by Rye Golf Club.

iii) Camber Sands

The line extension headed south-eastwards, and then east (in 1939) to Camber Sands station. This consisted of a wooden platform and run-round loop, with a shelter added later. A tea hut was located behind the original station site, which later became a pig sty!

Peter A Harding describes the station area as being like the Wild West, and I agree. I highly recommend Peter's booklet, not just to imagine the atmosphere of the line in operation, or simply to model it, but with a view to reopening it. As mentioned, the Rye & Camber Tramway is a railway which should be reborn. It would only need to begin with a 'Trust A' project (an investors' capital trust) to reopen a short stretch from a recreated Rye tram station site to Broadwater Stream, as part of an interactive museum about the line, with a possible later extension around Northpoint Beach as near to Golf Links Station as possible.

Chapter 8: Hastings Miniature Railway and the Cliff Railways

Hastings Miniature Railway

Lord Dowshire had a private miniature railway at Easthampstead Park, and it was the steam locomotives from there which went to the Hastings Miniature Railway. The HMR began in 1947, running on the beach at St Leonards, and was owned by the Ian Allan company. The following summer it extended to Hastings beach, opposite the Old Town. The fully working miniature steam locomotives were: GWR Saint 4-6-0, built 1938 (formerly N. 2943 Hampton Court, constructed by Trevor Guest); LMS Royal Scot Class, built 1938, No. 46100 in 1946; Firefly pannier 0-6-0 tank engine, built 1934 (rebuilt in 1946). During the 1980s the steam locomotives were replaced by a double-ended diesel locomotive in green (with a cab at both ends),

which was itself subsequently replaced by another diesel. That was also green in 1998, but is now painted blue, although it is still named 'Swee' Pea'. The line gauge is ten and a quarter inch.

The HMR was originally 250 yards long, but was extended around 1950, and again in 1959. Since then, the half mile line has started at its Marine Parade station beside the main coast road, opposite the Old Town near the west end of George Street. It has a small ticket office building with a single platform to its right, served by a run-round loop and

Loco 9-6-0 being prepared at the Hastings Miniature Railway, 8th April 1955. Photo: Norman Simmons (Hugh Davies/Photos From The Fifties)

track (with ticket hut) and an island platform between the two. If Hastings Council want to regenerate Hastings, they might like to consider extending the railway to the pier and then onto the pier itself, when it is rebuilt (see below). This would surely draw in more people. The Ian Allan Company also owned a narrow gauge line in Hastings' Alexandra Park (photo, page 77). By 2010 the new passing loop at the midway platform was in use, enabling two-train operation, although no second platform has yet been added.

Sadly, Hastings pier was almost 95% destroyed by fire

Loco 0-6-0 running tender-first at the Hastings Miniature Railway, 8th April 1955. Photo: Norman Simmons (Hugh Davies/Photos From The Fifties/)

The new passing loop on the Hastings Miniature Railway, 2010. Photo: Paul O'Callaghan

the main track. It passes various children's amusements (go-carting and boating pool, etc.) and then a coach and car park as it goes through an unnamed platform, before going through an engine shed, which doubles as a mock tunnel (with doors at either end to close it off at night, with the rolling stock housed within). The line then emerges in front of the East Cliff Lift southern station, passing over a right of way for cars, and then enters the station. The terminus has two tracks, with a platform to the right of the right hand

*Hastings Miniature Railway train with lady driver, 2010.
Photo: Paul O'Callaghan*

Hastings West Hill Lift Railway

This was the first of the two Lift railways in Hastings, located behind George Street, and links the West Hill and its castle to the Old Town. Its two 6 ft gauge tracks pass through a tunnel (118 ft high by 19 ft) for much of its length. It was opened on 25th March 1891 by the local MP. Three years later, the company went into liquidation, the railway being bought by Hastings Passenger Lift Ltd, which then sold it in April 1947 for £4,500 to Hastings council.

Entrance to the lower station at Hastings West Cliff Lift Railway, 2007. Photo: Paul O'Callaghan

The tunnel was dug to combine with an already existing cavern. The BoT inspector was none other than Major Hutchinson, who inspected ordinary railways, and he cleared the Lift line for opening. The engineers were F & J Plowman. Work began on the line in January 1889,

in 2010 (already having been closed since 2006), but it is halfway through obtaining funding for a rebuild, so an extension along the seafront to the pier would still be a good idea and would encourage more people visiting the Old Town to go there. Another miniature railway also exists beside the Eastbourne–Hampden Park line, open for simple rides around a lake.

costing £16,000, and the lower station was then constructed in red stone, built by contractors A H Holme & C W King. Each track has a separate carriage, seating twelve people, with standing room for four. Both are powered by diesel engines (the original gas ones having been replaced in 1924) and are linked to winding gear, with the winding wheel located in the upper station. This was converted to an electric system in 1971. The railway was refurbished in 1991.

Hastings East Hill Lift Railway

Undoubtedly, given a choice between this lift railway and the West Hill option, most people flock to this one, given that much of its rival is less spectacularly contained within a tunnel. Originally, the Hastings Lift Company had wanted to build this line whilst their West Hill one was still under construction. The Hastings Corporation said no, but later built the line themselves.

The Cliff face had to be dug out for the tracks, necessitating the removal of 2,400 yards of soil. The two tracks are both 5 ft gauge and 267 ft in length. The lower station building is built in a cottage style using Portland stone, and contains a waiting room and toilets. The upper station is built to resemble a castle.

The two carriages were built of wood and could carry 20 people. The line was originally powered by a water balance system, the water provided by two tanks located in each of the two mock towers of the upper station. A tank beside the lower station collected the water, with a crossover pulley system below it. The tanks contained up to 600 gallons of water. Once filled at the top station, the system would release the water through pipes as the carriage descended. This was replaced with electric winding gear in 1973-4 for £35,000, following a water pump failure. It revived for only a short time before closing for further work in September 1974, reopening again in September 1976. During this period

Hastings East Cliff Railway in action, 2010. Photo: Paul O'Callaghan

The East Cliff Lift Railway, with Hastings Miniature Railway in the foreground, August 1998. Photo: Paul O'Callaghan

two new carriages were installed for a price of £6,900 each, being 8 ft wide and with double-sealed doors, although the passenger capacity was reduced from 20 to a maximum of 16 people.

In June 2007, the East Hill lift was struck by lightning, forcing its temporary closure for repairs. On the day it reopened, one of the lifts failed to stop and crashed into the buffers of the lower station, whilst the other lift consequently indented itself into the upper building by eight inches. Windows were smashed in both buildings. Four people, including a young girl who needed help for shock, were aboard the lower lift. It was the first incident of its kind. The line was immediately closed for investigation and finally opened again in 2010.

Chapter 9: The Eastbourne Tramway

Background

The story of the Eastbourne Tramway is one of a tram enthusiast who managed to set up his own line, only to be chased off by council paranoia and encroaching road building schemes.

In the 1880s the local council considered constructing a tramway to Pevensey, from Terminus Road to Seaside Road. It pondered it again in 1902, but opted for buses instead. Decades later, electrical and mechanical engineer Claude Lane, who already had his own business in Barnet, Hertfordshire, arrived on the scene and officially formed Modern Electric Tramways Ltd on 19th May 1953. He began the process of trying to find a permanent home for a tramway operation, having spent the previous few years running demonstration services at festivals, including a season at St Leonards in 1951. Having moved to North Wales, he had eventually set up a tramway at Rhyl, but was unhappy with it. At the end of 1953, therefore, Lane began searching for a new site. He began a plan to move the line to Folkestone, but a trustee of the chosen site vetoed this.

Captain Howey of the Romney, Hythe & Dymchurch Railway had offered Lane the chance of running his trams on the RHDR, but Lane was after more. When passing through Eastbourne one night in his car, Lane stopped at a garage and enquired of the attendant where he was. He was told that he was beside the Crumbles beach (and, as the area was then, a firing range), and the location piqued his

Original postcard showing 'tramcars passing at miniature golf course' on the Eastbourne Tramway, early 1960s. (Paul O'Callaghan collection)

interest. Due to his experiences at nearby St Leonards, where he had been able to set up a tramway for just one season, Lane was in doubt as to whether or not to try his luck in Eastbourne, but his colleague Allan Gardner encouraged him to proceed. In May 1953 they contacted Eastbourne Council, and on 17th and 18th September operated their trams on a demonstration track for council officers to observe and ride upon. One of them was George Hill, who was very impressed with the tramway.

Unlike at St Leonards, this time, on 13th November 1959, Lane obtained an agreement from the council for more than one season, with a five-year contract to operate trams from the period 1st April 1954 to 31st March 1959, which included the construction of a depot. The Eastbourne Tramway finally opened on 4th July 1954, while a new family business took over Lane's Rhyl line.

The Rhyl Tramway had been 15 inches in gauge, but Eastbourne Tramway would be 2 ft gauge, albeit still using flat-bottomed rail as at Rhyl. The agreement was for the line to operate from the gates at Princess Park northwards, and then westwards into the park (north of the pond), before proceeding northwards again to Wartling Road, where the depot was built. 230 yards of the agreed track had been laid from the depot to the Golf House (the halfway point) by opening day, and the tramway was then opened southwards to the Gates terminus on 15th August 1954. The agreement also covered a shelter and sales kiosk being erected at the Gates terminus, along with an emergency generator. The Mayor opened the line by driving tram car No. 226 along the whole length of the line, with other local officials riding onboard. The traditional speeches associated with railway openings then followed at the tramway depot. The BBC filmed the event and subsequently broadcast it twice over the next couple of days. The initial fare in 1955, from Royal Parade to Golf House, was 1 1/2 d (old pence). The price for a tram from the depot to Royal Parade was 3 d.

Extension of the Tramway

In January 1956, following a good sales season, Lane applied to the council's Entertainment & Pleasure Boards Committee for permission to extend the line by 330 yards so that it ran fully onto the Crumbles. Permission was at first rejected, as on 18th January 1956 the Committee had notified Lane's company that they proposed to extend the Royal Parade road to connect with Wartling Road, which meant that it would twice cross the tramway. The track would also have to be moved further towards the coastline, away from the Gates terminus, to allow the road to be laid in the tramway's place. A new depot would also be required, as the existing one would be isolated from the road, 320 yards east

of it. Permission for the replacement depot was obtained, and it was planned to include a shop and exhibition area, but these aspects were not eventually included.

On 17th February 1956, Claude Lane attended the next meeting of the Committee to try once again to gain permission for his Crumbles extension, and this time he was successful, at first obtaining a general consent. However, on 20th April the Committee's permission was clarified to mean that he could openly extend the line by 320 yards. The five-year agreement for operating the existing tramway was also extended until 19th October 1960. On 19th October 1956, the Committee agreed a further extension of the contract until 31st October 1963. The Mayor returned on the Whitsun Monday in 1956 to open the tramway again for that season's operation, and stop and request stops were placed along the route. In December 1956, the application for permission to double the track between Golf House and the depot was submitted to the Committee and was granted, with work beginning immediately.

At this point, however, the nearby Chatsworth Estate unexpectedly claimed that the land upon which the extension was being built had in fact been gifted by the estate to the council - with conditions. The estate was annoyed that it had not been consulted on the line expansion and took revenge for this snub (as there were no technical grounds on which

Tram on the double track section of the Eastbourne Tramway, 1964. The tram depot can been in the far distance. Photo: Mick Funnell

to deny it) by objecting. While the council attempted to sort this out, all work on the new track ceased. Eventually it was discovered that the Crumbles extension didn't actually go onto the gifted estate area, and in fact remained on council land. Despite this, it did come very close to the boundary with the gifted land, so the estate put in a further objection to block it. In the end, a compromise was reached whereby the extension would be laid 15 yards away from the boundary, forcing Lane to have to lift the new track and re-

lay it, which delayed opening of the extended line. This site is close to where the Sovereign Leisure Centre stands today.

The extension was opened on 24th May 1958. Mayor J W G Howlett performed the usual honours by driving No. 6 tram car from the depot to the new Crumbles track and then back, before going all the way to the Gates terminus. Then the ceremonies moved back to the depot where the Mayor gave a speech and was presented with a framed picture of himself driving the tram earlier in the day. BBC TV had again turned up to film the event, using the same tram as before (225) and filmed Howlett at the controls. The recording was transmitted the following Wednesday.

A new workshop and administration office (with bed facilities for Lane) was also built in 1958, costing £2,000, and was served by a branch from the tramway. Lane closed his Barnet works with a view to concentrating all his activities in one spot.

Problems Arise

In September 1959, an attempt was made to gain permission for a line extension to Langney Point (where Martello Tower 66 still stands), but the Eastbourne Corporation's Transport Manager, a Mr Canon, objected, as he thought the 'toy' tramway was attempting to become a rival public service! He assumed the line would try to compete with the

Corporation's bus routes, ultimately replacing trams with its own buses. The decision was postponed for twelve months in November 1959, so Lane asked for permission to extend the other way, from Gates to Redoubt, stating that as his fares were higher than the bus fares, he couldn't in any case compete with the Corporation. However, the decision on this extension was also deferred.

In October, Lane's company asked for its contract to be extended beyond 1963, but this was refused, as was permission for the extension to Langney Point. Mr Canon continued to fear that the tramway would be a source of competition and wanted the council to impose restrictions. In particular, he was afraid that Claude Lane's company would sell shares to Southdown Motor Services. There was an agreement already standing that the Southdown company would not operate buses in the Borough of Eastbourne, giving the Corporation a monopoly on bus services (which were only deregulated in 1986), but a shareholder alliance with the tramway could potentially give it a back-door method of directly threatening Corporation buses. Canon's fears also made sense in that once the tramway was outside the Borough, a Southdown-affiliated company could, in theory, have been able to run its trams up to the northern terminus, where passengers might have continued on into Eastbourne. The missing element of these concerns,

however, was that there was never any evidence that Claude Lane and his company ever planned to do such a thing; they just wanted to run a tramway. But the likes of Mr Canon remained worried.

As time went by, progress began to feel uphill for the Eastbourne Tramway in general. In December 1960, the line tried to obtain permission for an extension of just ten yards, but even that was refused. Lane had by now assessed that he would be able to get permission from the Chatsworth Estate for the extension to Langney Point, but this made no

Tram crossing on the Eastbourne Tramway, near the gasworks (just visible in the distance, far left), 1964. Photo: Mick Funnell

difference. A year later, in December 1961, half a mile of overhead cable was stolen, worth the then substantial price of £40. In addition, local yobs were beginning to throw pebbles at the overhead traction poles, just to listen to the interesting noise they made. Lane would personally chase them off (although today he'd most likely be the one locked up for harassment!).

In September 1964, the Committee gave Lane just one year's extension on his contract (so that it could now end on 31st October 1965). Lane approached the Committee in September 1965 for a seven-year extension on his contract, to make it financially worthwhile to improve the tramway. Relaying just 150 yards of track had cost £300, and by now most of the track was 11 years old and needed renewing.

At this point, the Town Clerk was told by the Borough Surveyor of plans for proposed new roads in the Crumbles area, and related them to the Committee members - and to Claude Lane, who was shocked to hear of this development. The Committee suggested the tramway be moved southwards, but Lane retorted that the council should instead support his extensions to Langney Point and Redoubt. At a meeting in October, attended by Lane and his solicitor, the issue of the tramway potentially selling out to a bus company was again raised by the Committee. Consequently, the meeting offered the company a contract

extension of just three years, furthering it to 31st October 1968 on condition of the track being moved, under the direction of the Borough Surveyor.

On 16th February 1966, Lane returned to the Committee with his solicitor to give notice that the October agreement was not acceptable, but the council would not budge. As a result, Lane attempted to come up with a new proposal - but then heard the Town Clerk was no longer supporting the tramway, and indeed was influencing others in their decisions.

In March 1966, Lane accepted an agreement for a short extension of the line operation, on the condition that he didn't have to move his workshop (which the Corporation had wanted relocated) during the summer of 1966, and on the grounds that the legal right lay with Lane's company to terminate the agreement on expiry of notice. Perceiving the likely outcome, Lane began searching for a new home for his tramway around this time.

The Final Years

In October 1966, the Borough Surveyor revealed more details of the new road scheme to the Committee. Only the Crumbles to the depot section of the tramway would have been unaffected by it. The Committee informed the Town Clerk to give notice to the tramway company that the track must be moved by 31st October 1967. However, on 10th

The Eastbourne Tramway at Princes Park, 1964. Photo: Mick Funnell

February 1967, the road building was deferred for a year, leaving the tramway able to operate for another season until 31st October 1968. A further delay in road laying followed: the Sussex River Authority had to reconstruct the Crumbles outfall, but couldn't do this for another year, enabling the tramway to be granted one last year of operation, up until 31st October 1969. During the final weeks, the trams carried posters stating, 'Last Tram Weeks', and ultimate closure came on 14th September 1969.

From hereon, everything had to be quickly dismantled and carried off by lorry to Seaton in Devon, where the Eastbourne Tramway was reborn as the Seaton Tramway, along the old branch line, reopening in sections from 1970. Sadly, after only the first section of the new tramway was opened, Claude Lane died. Today, you can still travel on the Eastbourne trams, but beside the River Axe from Seaton to Colyford's old station, instead of beside the sea. (One can't help hoping that Lane has been reincarnated somewhere nearby, so that he can travel on his own tramway.)

Back in Sussex, the Marshtello Railways Association continues to have a long-term aim (one which has thus far taken over ten years to achieve) of having another miniature tramway at Eastbourne, operating from the Harbour to Redoubt, Pier and Holywell, replacing the 'Dotto' train. The Dotto is a motorised car in the shape of a train, which pulls 'carriages' along the Eastbourne seafront from just short of the Marina to the beginning of the cliffs at Holywell. Perhaps ironically, it is operated by the local bus company.

Aircraft Factory Line

There was one last small railway near the vicinity of the Eastbourne Tramway: this operated inside an aircraft factory, installed to move seaplanes from the factory to the shore. Fuel for this industrial line probably came from the BP siding.

Chapter 10: Hall & Co. Narrow Gauge Line

The Hall & Co. Line

In 1932, having ceased using shingle for the development of Eastbourne, the latest Duke of Devonshire allowed Hall & Co. (which gained a lease for the shingle) to lay a 2 ft gauge track a mile long, upon which two diesel Simplex locomotives hauled wagons. Shingle was collected at one end and put into a new machine at the other, which sifted

Hall & Co. rails laid on top of the disused Crumbles branch trackbed, 1950.
Photo: J J Smith (Bob Cookson collection)

Hunslet loco No.46 on the Hall & Co. line, 1955.
Photo: Sid C Nash (Bob Cookson collection)

the shingle into separately-sized loads. From here these were transported by lorries.

This railway operated until 1964, between the Crumbles Branch track bed and the main road. The photos from the collection of Bob Cookson (as seen above) reveal that Hall & Co. in fact recycled Crumbles Branch track by using the same sleepers in-situ, simply laying their narrow gauge rails between the old standard gauge rails.

Railway worker gang on the Hall & Co. line, spring 1950.
Photo: Bob Cookson collection

The Royal Artillery Line

Another railway once ran near here from 1874, and was used by the Royal Artillery for experiments (when they were not blowing up the Martello Towers!). It was laid on the coast side of Pevensey Road, to Anthony Hill from the end of the Crumbles Branch. Beyond Anthony Hill it headed west to Martello Tower 68 and then east to Langney Point.

Chapter 11: Volks Electric Railway and the 'Daddy Long Legs' Line

Volks Electric Railway

Probably the most famous of the Sussex narrow gauge lines is the still surviving Volks Electric Railway at Brighton (or, more accurately, Volk's – although signs at the line itself now omit the apostrophe). Today, the Volks line runs from the Aquarium (east of the current pier) to Black Rock (where the Marina begins), and attracts thousands of visitors every year. It is one and a quarter miles in length and runs beside the sea wall and along the actual beach.

Created by Magnus Volk, son of a German clockmaker, by the start of 1883 he had already installed electric lighting in his native Brighton (at the Pavilion), and then requested permission from the Brighton Corporation to establish a 2 ft gauge electric passenger railway along the beach at Maderia Drive. After overcoming objections from some locals, concerned about the impact the line might have on their neighbourhood, it was quickly constructed and opened by the Mayor on 4th August 1883.

'The Volks' had the distinction of being the very first electric railway in Britain. Originally just quarter of a mile in length, running from the Aquarium (today the Sea Life Centre) to the site of the now lost Chain Pier, gas engines and electric dynamos powered the line's first 12 ft trains. Volk soon requested permission to extend the line to Hove, but when the Corporation refused this, Volk instead asked to extend the line eastwards to Paston Place (today's halfway point), to which it agreed. Volk was granted the use of Paston Place Arch, a cave dug out for a pumping system in the early 19th century, which he turned into his office.

The station at Paston Place was then called Banjo Groyne, with a request stop halfway between it and the Aquarium. The extension opened on 4th April 1884, while the original

Train at Volks Electric Railway, 2009. Photo: Andy Thomas

line remained closed awhile for reconstruction and eventual joining with the new track. The gauge was expanded to 2 ft, 8 and a half inches, and Kerr, Stuart & Co. supplied the rails. The railway carriages had a speed of up to 30 mph, but usually went no more than 10 mph. Like many earlier train carriages, they were made from mahogany wood and were highly decorated. A new gas engine was installed at the power plant for the revamped line, which ran at 40 amps.

In contrast to most successful line openings, the smooth running of the Volks extension ceremonies was spoiled when the weight of the dignitaries in the official VIP train caused its springs to press down to the frame, locking the carriage onto the wood of the level crossing. Rival horse-drawn cab drivers jeered at the collapse. Despite this setback, the new extension opened to the public on 7th April. As for the jeering, the Volks line would be assailed by a number of objectors for a while, as it suffered local vandalism (not by yobs, but allegedly by fishermen and cab drivers concerned about the impact on their trade). The elements, unsurprisingly, also threatened the line, as several storms damaged the tracks throughout the 1890s (a hazard which continues into the 21st century, of course). Other setbacks occurred as the decades went by, as the hazards of electric lines became apparent. A number of accidents and even fatalities, some involving children, wet dogs, and a horse

ABOVE: Aquarium Station, Volks Railway, 2002.   BELOW: The eastern terminus at Marina Station (Black Rock), 2002. Photos: Paul O'Callaghan

(electrocuted when it stood on a level crossing), necessitated stronger safety measures. But somehow the line weathered all of these challenges.

Under a new Brighton Electric Railway (BER) agreement with the Corporation (which allowed for the removal of the line on its orders), Volk was permitted to further deviate the line and create an improved station at Paston Place, while rent was not required until 1902. Instead of the BoT inspecting the line, Volk had to have it examined by the Corporation's surveyor.

In 1900, Volk proposed to extend the line further east to Black Rock, to make up for the expected loss of the Brighton & Rottingdean Seashore Electric Tramway (see below) due to sea defence work. When the latter did close, Volk further proposed to extend the BER to Rottingdean but, despite gaining an Act of Parliament to do this, he couldn't raise the £40,000 required before the Act's stipulated time of completion. Volk did, however, get his extension to Black Rock, built on a wooden viaduct with steel braces. When the tide was in, there was quite a spectacle as the train passed over the sea, with waves crashing below it, although over the years the viaduct was gradually buried in shingle. The Black Rock extension station, which opened in May 1901, was originally a wooden shed, before being improved with new buildings in 1911. Following completion of the Palace Pier in 1901, the western Aquarium terminus was renamed after the pier.

A new western terminus was eventually built, slightly further east of the original one, and opened on 27th June 1930, largely due to the widening of the main road (a bathing pool had also been proposed, which would have forced the railway's closure, but the widening of the road and the reduction of the line was agreed as a compromise). However, even that slight move away from the pier meant that the revenue from the line promptly dropped by a fifth.

Although by now there were 50 employees and ten carriages, more setbacks followed. Just thirteen days after the railway's 50th birthday, at which Magnus Volk was hailed and a new carriage presented to him, Volk died. His son took over the company for a time, and in 1937 a bathing pool opened at Black Rock, which did bring in more custom, but under the Brighton Corporation (Transport) Act of 1938, the Corporation took control of the line's operation on 1st April 1940. One of Volk's other sons (an author) commented how merciful it was that his father wasn't around to see this happen. Three days later, the beach was entirely closed by the Government due to the threat of Nazi invasion. Bizarrely, the termini were completely demolished and the railway was left to rot.

However, after the war the Corporation repaired the line and, happily, Volks Electric Railway lived again, reopening on 15th May 1948. The western terminus gained an old tramway shelter as a station building, and upside down umbrella-shaped canopies were installed at Paston Place and Black Rock.

In 1963 a doomed proposal was put forward to re-extend the line back to the pier, but the cost ultimately outweighed the potential income. In 1965 a futuristic monorail was put forward as an idea to replace the Volks, but this was also rejected. Complaints about the line's condition began to

Paston Place Station, Volks Railway, showing the depot, 2002.
Photo: Paul O'Callaghan

Crossing at Volks Electric Railway, 2002. Photo: Paul O'Callaghan

1983 as part of the celebrations.

The shingle-buried wooden viaduct of the Marina extension was replaced by a concrete structure, and, in 1994, a pumping house facility for storing water caused by storms was built beside the line's eastern end, next to the Marina's new and current platform. Further work has been carried out since and, with alternative plans seemingly abandoned, it would seem that Volks Electric Railway is here to stay for the time being, with the line still cherished by many rail enthusiasts.

Train at Paston Station, Volks Electric Railway, 2009. Photo: Andy Thomas

mount in the 1970s, and the council regarded it as being unable to cope with an expected increase in passengers from the new Brighton Marina project of 1975. In 1981, youths used petrol bombs to destroy the station at Black Rock, although the council did rebuild it. The railway was then nearly replaced by an automatic Maglev (magnetic levitation) railway system, with plans to move the existing line to a park! The decision of what to do was postponed until after the Volks celebrated its 100 years (attended by Volk's youngest son). Black Rock was renamed Marina in

The 'Daddy Long Legs' Line: The Brighton & Rottingdean Seashore Electric Tramroad

In addition to his more famous electric tramway, Magnus Volk also founded another Brighton line, now long-lost. Known officially as the Brighton & Rottingdean Seashore Electric Tramroad, it is perhaps best remembered by its nickname, the 'Daddy Long Legs' line. When the tide was in, raised trams ran through the sea, their wheels on concrete rails below the water. They were literally carriages on huge stilts, or, to put it another way, looked like pieces of a pier travelling through water, complete with lifebuoy rings. The line was built as the cheaper option for Volk to achieve his ambition of having a railway reach Rottingdean, as it was too costly to extend the Brighton Electric Railway up over the cliffs.

In 1893, Volk officially posited the idea of a tram running between piers through water at high tide, powered by an overhead cable held up by posts fixed into the beach. A railway inspector and other researchers spent some time playing with a model of the proposed line, and a new company was established, with local officials on its board. It required an Act of Parliament (of 23rd July 1893) to have it built, with part of the Act stipulating that the Brighton Corporation would have a legal right to divert or remove the line if so desired. The finances to build the line were

Tramcar 'Pioneer' heads off for Rottingdean on the appropriately nicknamed 'Daddy Long Legs' line. Photo: Chris Horlock collection

stipulated at £20,000, but the price was to go up almost another £30,000, and a further Act of Parliament was needed to extend the time within which the line had to be completed. The track was 2 ft 8 and a half inches, laid during the four hours of the day and the four hours of the night when the tide was out.

There were two sets of rails, and four sets of wheels at each corner of the trams, moving between the rails. The wheels were protected in steel plates. Four 24 ft legs (like pier pillars) extended from the steel-covered wheels to the deck of the tram, which had a cabin saloon with a mini-staircase leading up to it. The line ran from a pier at Paston Place. When the railway inspector came, he tested a tram at both high and low

Tramcar at the 'Banjo Groyne' terminus. Photo: Chris Horlock collection

tides to see how well it performed in pushing obstacles off the line. Each day, a qualified ship's captain was required to approve the conditions to see whether the tram could run.

On 28th November 1896, the tramway opened, if to limited effect. The service at high tide operated at a crawling speed, and only a little faster at low tide. When a storm hit in early December 1896 it wrecked the line and, despite the tramcar 'Pioneer' being strapped to the pier, this managed to break away, trundling through the stormy waves before toppling over. (How many times have trams been overturned by the sea..?) Seven months later, the line was reopened.

Whilst some people were undoubtedly too frightened to go on the 'Daddy Long Legs' line, it did at first prove a major tourist attraction. However, by 1900, less people were travelling on it, sea defences were causing the waves to damage the tracks, and the Brighton Corporation wanted to move part of the line (between Paston Place and Black Rock) further out to sea. Volk proposed to move his west-based terminus to the east, but the Corporation would not wait and, in January 1901, began ripping up the track. The line closed due to a mixture of all these problems and was finally dismantled in 1910. Some of the concrete blocks for the rails can still be seen on the beach at low tide, a reminder of a curious folly from earlier times.

Chapter 12: The Cuckmere Valley Railway

The Early Years

From the early 1930s, a 2 ft narrow gauge railway was constructed to move sand, pebbles and shingle from the Cuckmere estuary, between Seaford and Beachy Head. The line replaced the usage of the 'cut' canal, a straight channel dug in 1846 to by-pass the famous meander of the River Cuckmere. On 16th September 1933, A F Smith Ltd had requested permission from the local Catchment Board for a draft lease to construct a railway from New Wharf (at the estuary) to Exceat Bridge, which carries the main A259 road. (The line's goods yard is today occupied by the visitors' car park on the south side of the road, which serves the Exceat Visitor Centre.)

Initially it was ruled that 700 hundred tons

Loading hopper at the Cuckmere Valley Railway, date unknown. Photo: Lawson Little/Narrow Gauge Railway Society

of shingle would be allowed to be taken by the company, but this was changed to 4,000 cubic yards a week at a meeting on 9th June 1932, with the full licence being issued in 1933. An Orenstein Koppel locomotive is believed to have been used in the early years. When World War Two broke out, the military may have temporarily removed the track.

Exceat loco shed on the Cuckmere Valley Railway, date unknown. Photo: Lawson Little/Narrow Gauge Railway Society

The Post-War Period

A new agreement to restart the Cuckmere operation was made on 27th February 1950, using what was now described as a 'tramway'. On 23rd August, A F Smith leased the wharf, building and Exceat bridge for £20 and track was re-laid at the south end, while passing loops were created near the estuary. In this post-war period, two Simplex diesel locomotives operated the main line, with one locomotive ready as a spare, and by 1952 two Ransome & Rapier locomotives hauled 21 Hudson-type tipper wagons at a speed of just 10 mph. Operation eventually ceased in 1964. After the track was removed, it was reused by the National Rivers Authority (NRA) at Pevensey Bay.

Simplex Diesel (4WD) No. 8659 at the Cuckmere Valley Railway. Photo: Lawson Little/Narrow Gauge Railway Society

Several photos of the railway can be found at the Newhaven Local and Maritime Museum, most East Sussex libraries, the Seaford Collection and at the useful Narrow Gauge Railway Society.

Whilst most of the trackbed may well now be covered by the cycle path (which closely follows the course of the old line), other visible signs of the former railway may well remain for the eagle-eyed. Just where the river comes in towards the east, northwest of old Combe Bottom, there is a small stream. Over this is a tiny bridge with

Bridge in the Cuckmere Valley, 2007 - the last remains of the railway? Photo: Paul O'Callaghan

two rails, a narrow gauge width apart. So this may be the one last remnant of the Cuckmere Valley railway!

*

So concludes this two-volume exploration of East Sussex's coastal railways, with their many intriguing stations, branches, sidings and complex histories. Visitors are encouraged to seek out both the still-existing lines and the sites of long-removed railways, which continue to fascinate train enthusiasts and the public alike - hopefully these books will have whetted the appetite to find out more.

APPENDIX: Additional Photographs

In addition to the many fascinating photographs throughout this book, a few more are featured here which didn't find a home in the main layout, but which are of interest in their own right, plus a few station images not originally included in Volume 1 for reasons of space.

Crossing at the miniature gauge railway at Alexandra Park, Hastings, 2007. Photo: Paul O'Callaghan

Boynal 0-4-ST loco 'Mercede' on the Brede Valley Waterworks Railway, Hastings, date unknown. Photo: Hastings Library

ABOVE: Waves lap the narrow gauge railway at Winchelsea beach.
BELOW: Rye Harbour's Simplex loco. Photos: Hastings Library

ABOVE: Bishopstone Beach Halt (closed 1942), as seen in 1969. Photo:
John Scrace. BELOW: Seaford station, 2002. Photo: Paul O'Callaghan

ABOVE: Loco 32636, Newhaven West Quay, 1950. Photo: R C Riley
BELOW: West Quay line ruins in 2008. Photo: Paul O'Callaghan

ABOVE: Old construction rails, Hastings, 2010. Photo: Paul O'Callaghan
BELOW: Loco 32678, Breakwater, West Quay, 1963. Photo: R C Riley

(Volume 1) - ABOVE: Hampden Park Station, 1976. Photo: John Scrace
BELOW: Inside Hampden Park signal box. Photo: Roger Quantrill

(Volume 1) - ABOVE: Snailham, 1950s. Photo: Lens of Sutton collection
BELOW: Steam railmotor at Eastbourne. Photo: Bob Cookson collection

About the Author

Paul O'Callaghan was born in New Eltham, London, and moved to Eastbourne in 2005. He first became interested in railways around 1986.

In 1994, when leaving sixth form, Paul O'Callaghan had three options: to go into journalism; join the Police (his preferred option); or do science and biology courses and train to be a doctor. Instead, he was struck down by a disabling infection, which damaged his balance organs.

The legal battle to obtain official treatment for the condition has robbed Paul's mother of their house, and he still suffers from constant rocking vertigo. He was finally diagnosed with paresis of the inner ear and vestibular neuronitis in 2002, but no treatment was offered and the extent of the damage remains uninvestigated. After many years of trying to find his own treatment, Paul is now too old to undertake medical training, and journalism will be hazardous, as too many hours are spent at computers. Paul has instead been campaigning for funds to set up his own health and research centre for the medically neglected, although he still hasn't given up hope of becoming a police officer.

Despite all this, Paul has managed to have articles published in local railway and history newsletters, books and railway magazines, as well as a local history journal, in which he has also had photos published. A dozen draft pages from this book were displayed at the Marshlink Rail Festival in September 2007.

Alexander Forbes

Paul O'Callaghan

C3 2307 on the gasworks line, Crumbles branch, 19th February 1949. Photo: J J Smith (Bob Cookson collection)

S B Publications

S B Publications has numerous titles which cover in further detail many of the areas and places touched on in these pages. Information on these can be found at:

www.sbpublications.co.uk

Or contact us at: 14 Bishopstone Road, Seaford, East Sussex, BN25 2UB
Tel: 01323 893498 Email: *sbpublications@tiscali.co.uk*